Harvard University
Center for International Affairs

Executive Committee

Created in 1958, the Center for International Affairs fosters advanced study of basic world problems by scholars from various disciplines and senior officials from many countries. The research of the Center focuses on economic, social, and political development; the management of force in the modern world; the problems and relations of advanced industrial societies; transnational processes and international order; and technology and international affairs.

The Harvard Studies in International Affairs, which are listed at the back of this book, may be ordered from the Publications Office, Center for International Affairs, 6 Divinity Avenue, Cambridge, Mass. 02138, at the prices indicated. Recent books written under the auspices of the Center, listed on the last pages, may be obtained from bookstores or ordered directly from the publishers.

The Center is happy to provide a forum for the expression of responsible views. It does not, however, necessarily agree with them.

1

About the Author _____

Crispin Tickell is a member of the British Diplomatic Service. He has served in The Hague, Mexico, Paris and London, where he was Private Secretary to successive Cabinet Ministers. He has many interests, from pre-Columbian history to anthropology, and has contributed to various publications, including *Life After Death* (1976) with Arnold Toynbee and Arthur Koestler. He wrote the present book during his time at Harvard as a Fellow at the Center for International Affairs (1975-76) and the views expressed are of course strictly his own. He is now the Chef de Cabinet to the President of the Commission of the European Communities in Brussels.

L

CLIMATIC CHANGE AND WORLD AFFAIRS

HARVARD STUDIES
IN INTERNATIONAL AFFAIRS
Number 37

CLIMATIC CHANGE AND WORLD AFFAIRS

by Crispin Tickell

Foreword to this edition
by Lord Zuckerman
of Burnham Thorpe, O.M., K.C.B., F.R.S.

Foreword to the original edition
by Paul Doty

PERGAMON PRESS

Oxford · New York · Toronto
Sydney · Paris · Frankfurt

U.K.	Pergamon Press Ltd., Headington Hill Hall, Oxford OX2 0BW, England
U.S.A.	Pergamon Press Inc., Maxwell House, Fairview Park, Elmsford, New York 10523, U.S.A.
CANADA	Pergamon of Canada Ltd., 75 The East Mall, Toronto, Ontario, Canada
AUSTRALIA	Pergamon Press (Aust.) Pty. Ltd., 19a Boundary Street, Rushcutters Bay, N.S.W. 2011, Australia
FRANCE	Pergamon Press SARL, 24 rue des Ecoles, 75240 Paris, Cedex 05, France
FEDERAL REPUBLIC OF GERMANY	Pergamon Press GmbH, 6242 Kronberg-Taunus, Pferdstrasse 1, Federal Republic of Germany

British Library Cataloguing in Publication Data

Tickell, Crispin
Climatic change and world affairs.
1. Climatic changes - History
I. Title
551.6   QC981.8.C5   76-52230
ISBN 0-08-022228-5

*Printed in Great Britain by William Clowes & Sons Limited
London, Beccles and Colchester*

CONTENTS

FOREWORD TO THIS EDITION
by LORD ZUCKERMAN OF BURNHAM THORPE
O.M., K.C.B., F.R.S.

Not long after the Lord had gathered the waters in one place, and had caused dry land to appear—that is to say not long after, if measured by the pages of Genesis—Noah was forced to take to his ark because new floods covered all the earth. Then came a time when Moses, searching for a land where milk and honey still flowed, had to lead his flock across what we now know were man-made deserts. There was also a Tower of Babel, where men spoke in many tongues, without understanding, and heeding no message.

All this could only have happened in what was an infinitesimal fraction of the time that life has existed on this globe of ours, and in the course of which the surface of the earth has altered time and again out of all recognition. The shapes of continents and oceans have been continually changing; mountain ranges have thrust to the skies and then disappeared; and ice has covered the land. Relatively speaking it was not long before man as we know him emerged—at most a million out of more than four billion years since there was living matter—that the Bering Straits formed to separate the eastern tip of the Eurasiatic continent from America, and the Mediterranean to separate Europe from Africa. Only 5000 years ago, the Straits of Dover, which now separate us from France, was dry land. We may have a sense of the physical forces that have been at work, but we certainly do not wind the clock which triggers major changes in geography and in climate. All we know is that these forces are still there; that our earth is still changing; that the axis on which the globe spins every twenty-four hours is not immutably stable; that the orbit in which we move annually round the sun is not constant; that the sun from which the earth derives its energy is itself subject to change; that the climate we know—the winds, the rains, the seasons—is also changing from year to year.

In his brilliant short book, and with the clarity that marks the informed professional diplomat, Crispin Tickell sets our species, *Homo sapiens*, in the dimension of geological time. Those who have not been too bemused by science fiction should read and ponder. The first half of our century probably enjoyed a warmer climate than did any corresponding period in the past thousand years. In the 17th century, a drop in average temperature of only 1°C brought about a "little ice-age". A shift of a few degrees upwards could one day lead to the melting of the polar ice caps and the inundation of vast areas; one downwards to another age in which the land on which we live would be buried under hundreds of feet of ice.

If all this is something which is hard to comprehend, we should at least remind ourselves that in recent years many regions of the globe have suffered acute droughts, tornadoes and floods, and that many countries have suffered ruinous crop failures. We should also recognize that in his multiplying millions, man, and not "nature" on its own, is now affecting his physical environment in unpredictable ways. The world's climate seems to be moving into a phase of rapid change. And we need to realize that the units of time in which we make our social, economic and political decisions are incredibly small in comparison with those which affect climate. Nature's time-clock goes on ticking away, triggering unexpected changes, and as our physical environment changes, new political and economic strains and stresses develop in the world.

A vast amount still needs to be learnt about the factors which affect the earth's climate. But, as Crispin Tickell urges, it is now that we should begin to organize, on a worldwide scale, to monitor what is happening. It would be too late to do anything if, to take an extreme example, part of the ice which covers Greenland and which helps to anchor the northern ice cap were to break away. And undoubtedly we would be slow, and even reluctant, to recognize the first signs that anything like that was happening.

The problems of climate are clearly international. Man's present political problems are miniscule in relation to what could result from major changes in climate, and someone from outer space, viewing our globe in the units of geological time, could well suppose that nations of today behave like people who quarrel violently and murderously over immediate trivialities on the fiftieth floor of some huge Modern Tower of Babel, oblivious of the fact that it is blazing away merrily below them. It is not going to be easy to pool our understanding or to co-ordinate research into long-term climatic change; and it will be even more difficult to concert the actions which have to be taken to deal with suddden catastrophes—but in these matters the world cannot afford any Tower of Babel. One can only pray that the day will soon dawn when the current disputes and turmoil of national and international politics sink into the proper perspective of time; when speculations about man's future cease to be idle extrapolations about 'limits to growth'; and when we realise that in the context of real time, nature itself has been responsible for far more significant changes in the physical world within which living beings have evolved than any for which we, the human species, have been or are likely to be responsible.

July, 1977   S. ZUCKERMAN

FOREWORD

Much of the human condition results from the ways in which men divide their talents and energies between short-term, parochial problems and less urgent but more seminal threats to the continuation of global society. Perhaps the most pernicious consequence of the rapidity of change that marks the modern era is its mobilization of human thinking to deal almost solely with day-to-day accommodations to change; it ensures that tactics dominate strategy, that quick reaction triumphs over unhurried conception.

Yet through the miasma of temporal preoccupations some contrary trends are taking shape. Surely the view of the loneliness of the planet Earth as seen by space travelers, and now the desolateness of the Martian landscape, teach us of our total dependence on the thin biosphere we inhabit.

Some of industrial man's assaults on the biosphere are reversible, some are not—at least within centuries. It is increasingly evident that the most vulnerable aspect of the biosphere may be its climate. Over the ages, the temperature distribution in the biosphere has been maintained with only moderate fluctuations by a critical balance. Radiation coming from the sun and heat coming from inside the earth have been nicely balanced by the energy returned to space so as to energize the biosphere. A shift of 2°C in mean temperatures leads either to ice ages or to melting of the polar ice caps, either of which would now destroy much of present civilization. Lesser changes will convert farmland to deserts. The inadequacy of our understanding of the causative steps leading to this degree of change is alarming. This intensifies when we realize that the artificial production of energy at the earth's surface is now rising to the point where it can affect this delicate balance, and it is doubling every fifteen to twenty years.

We are in Mr. Tickell's debt that he has sensed the magnitude of possible climatic changes and inquired into their meaning for earth dwellers and their societies in the time scale of the human life span.

Paul Doty
Mallinckrodt Professor of Biochemistry

Director
Program for Science and International Affairs
Harvard University

INTRODUCTION

For the United States the winter of 1976/77, simultaneously spreading crippling cold in the East and Middle West and withering drought in the West, was a fearful experience. Even. earlier, small talk about the weather had turned into concern about the climate. Droughts, floods, heat waves and sudden chills unprecedented in living memory afflicted people used to an agreeably mixed climate, whose fluctuations had hitherto been so constant that real change had passed almost unnoticed. 1972 and 1974 were also perturbing years which cast long shadows over world agriculture. But the disasters they brought made fewer headlines, partly perhaps because they chiefly affected those to whom disasters were all too familiar, and partly because people seemed resistant to the idea of admitting a climatic variable into their calculations. Even those required to think about the future—farmers, economists, planners, and politicians—preferred to work on a simple extrapolation of today's here and now.

That has now begun to change. Worry about the climate has been added to other worries about the future. Indeed, it can be seen as one of the strands in the knot of problems involving multiplication of the human species, depletion of natural resources, pollution of the environment, and demands for higher living standards. Vulnerability to climatic change is increasingly recognized as a crucial element both in economic management within states and in relationships between them. In the United States the Central Intelligence Agency was one of the first to try and assess the political and economic implications for the shifting balance of world power. Our ability, deliberate or inadvertent, to cause climatic change, possibly to the detriment of others, is also a new and alarming development. Yet of all the aspects of the earth's environment, the climate and its variations, natural or otherwise, remain one of the least understood. It is an area where vital information is still lacking, where scientists can both passionately and plausibly disagree with each other, and where the man with a bee in his bonnet could still turn out to be right.

It seems nevertheless more than time to look with a somewhat political eye into the nature of the climate, why it works as it does, the causes of change, the extremes to which change can go, and the possible effects on mankind. On this basis we can consider the implications for present and future generations, and what if anything could—or should—be done. Such a study requires an excursion into science as well as international affairs, and a certain lengthening of the perspectives to which we are accustomed.

To stretch the understanding in this way needs a different focus of space and time. Those who fly high in aircraft can sometimes see the curve of the world, and the smallness of the atmospheric envelope around it. It amounts to no more than a film of moisture on a sphere, and its mass is less than a minute proportion of the earth as a whole. The passenger cannot of course look down beyond the shining surface into the sphere which is the ground of life. Nor can he see the successive layers of gas above which make life possible by giving protection from harmful radiation in space. Nor can he get any idea of the size of space from the blue sky. To say that the sun is no more than one suburban star in a galaxy of one hundred thousand million stars, and that this galaxy is no more than one among a hundred thousand million galaxies is to speak in abstractions. But we can have a sense of distance in our own backyard. If the sun is reduced to the size of an orange, the earth is a grain of sand at 30 feet, and the nearest star—another orange—is a thousand miles away.

The scale of time is even harder to grasp. When in the last

century a poet described the desert ruins of Petra as "rose-red city half as old as time," he meant it literally. For him absolute time began 4,000 years before Christ. For us relative time began with the universe we can see between 15,000 and 20,000 million years ago; and according to our calculations the earth was formed about 4,600 million years ago. Suppose we knock off the zeros and reduce 4,600 million years to 46 years (a good life span in most human history), then the dinosaurs died just over six months ago, the present human breed emerged about a week ago, our counting system before and after Christ began less than a quarter of an hour ago, and the Industrial Revolution has lasted just over a minute. More relevant to our present purposes, on the same time scale there were major ice ages on the earth nine and a half years, seven and three quarter years, six and a quarter years, four and a half years and around three years ago. The most recent series of glaciations began less than a week ago, and the last glaciers retreated about an hour ago.

In this perspective we live in a tiny, damp, curved space at a pleasantly warm moment. It is hard for those in temperate latitudes to imagine the climate they know as anything but pleasantly warm. If climate is defined as average weather over 40 years, then the warm conditions which prevailed in the northern hemisphere in the first half of this century were normal in their time. But in a time span of 500 years or longer, this warmth was distinctly abnormal. It was cooler before, and between 1945 and 1970 it became cooler again. Indeed the period 1900 to 1945 may have been the warmest in a thousand years.

These variations, assessed on averages, are pretty small: the differences can be measured in tenths of a degree Celsius (an increase of about 0.6°C. between 1800 and 1940, and a fall of about 0.3°C. since then). But they should not be dismissed as negligible. Air temperature is only one way of measuring a climate. Rise and fall by a few tenths of a degree may point to a vital shift in weather conditions, more or less sunshine or cloud, glaciation or warm wet winds. Each of the local temperatures which contribute to a statistical average may—and do—fluctuate drastically. In equatorial regions temperature is in any case less significant than incidence of rainfall. Most important, the range of variation between what we regard as extreme conditions is remarkably small. The average temperature in the northern hemisphere at the time of "the Little Ice Age" in the second half of the 17th century (when fairs took place on the frozen Thames) was probably only 1° to 2°C. less than at present, and even at the height of the last glaciation some 18,000 years ago (when most of the British Isles were under ice), the mean global difference was not more than 6°C. with greater or smaller changes in specific areas.[1]

Climate is constant only in its variability. But before we can consider why it should vary, we have to know how the weather works in that tiny, damp, curved space which is our living room.

It is not too difficult to describe the principles of the weather machine, but its precise mechanisms are of a complexity which have so far defied integrated analysis. No one has yet made a mathematical model capable of simulating the operation of more than a small part of it. In some ways the more it is studied the less we realize we know. For example, only in the last few years we have come better to appreciate the immense importance of the sea, which occupies more than two-thirds of the earth's surface, in conserving heat, conveying it from one area to another, and transferring it to the atmosphere in a way and according to rhythms not yet established.

Stated in the most simple terms, the power which drives the weather is the radiation of the sun and the spin of the earth on its own axis (for present purposes the energy which comes from the earth itself can be ignored). Of the sun's radiation, only part reaches and is absorbed by the surface of the earth. Some, including much of the dangerous shortwave ultraviolet radiation, is stopped or reflected back in the outer reaches of the atmosphere. Some is reflected back by cloud, dust, and other particles in the air. Some is reflected back by the surface of the earth: ice and desert are good reflectors, water and forest are good absorbers. The remaining radiation retained by the earth warms the atmosphere, but is eventually reradiated into space at relatively long wavelengths in the infrared. Without an equilibrium of radiation, or if the balance were to be interfered with, the earth would obviously become warmer or colder.

The sun's radiation falls differently according to the tilt of the earth. The equator and tropical regions receive most because there the sun's rays are most nearly vertical, and there is least atmosphere to dilute them. At the poles by contrast the rays are almost parallel to the surface, they have a long way to go through the atmosphere, and most of them are anyway bounced off the ice back into space. At the equator the earth receives more radiation than it returns; and at the poles (and over deserts) it returns more radiation than it receives. What turns the weather machine is the earth's adjustment to this imbalance through the transport of heat by wind and water from the equator towards the poles, and a corresponding movement of cold wind and water from the poles towards the equator. The precise way in which it does so is determined by the spin of the earth, coupled with the particular configuration of land, sea, and ice cap.

The familiar pattern of winds and currents is the result. In broad terms it produces a warm, wet, and stormy area on each side of the equator, an area of sunshine and sinking air where all the world's great deserts lie, the temperate areas in mid-latitudes governed by strong westerly winds, and the concentrations of ice and snow around the poles. No part of the weather system can be dissociated from any other: although the working parts have a certain tolerance, whatever happens in one area is likely sooner than later to have its effects around the world. The seasonal shifting of boundaries between the main areas is a function of the changing tilt of the earth towards the sun. It is these boundary areas which are most sensitive to climatic change. The behavior of the

Asiatic monsoon is an easy example: the shift of a few degrees northwards of stormy equatorial weather in the northern summer brings rain to India and southern Asia; it shifts
southwards again in the southern summer, and this time
covers northern Australia. On the extent of this seasonal
movement north and south, and on the tropical disturbances
within it, depend the lives of hundreds of millions of people.
   Seen from outer space the system would look fairly stable.
Seasonal changes might not be the same every year. Annual
temperatures might vary within a degree Celsius. Weather
patterns might wobble over a few degrees latitude or longitude. But by and large the machine would seem to tick over
with reassuring regularity. The trouble about this spaceman's
view is twofold: first, as we have seen, small changes can
matter a lot to those who experience them; and secondly, the
machine, from what we know of its past, is far from regular,
and—depending on the time we take to look at it—can radically change its manner of operation. The point was well put
in 1969:

> . . . One can imagine a gambler's die lying on the floor
> of a truck running over a rough road; the die is stable on
> any of its six faces so that in spite of bounding and vibra-
> tion the same face usually remains up—until a particu-
> larly big bump jars it so that it lands with a different face
> up, whereupon it is stable in its new position . . . Per-
> haps in recent years we have been bouncing along with,
> say, a four showing. Perhaps 200 years ago the die
> flipped over to three for a moment, then flipped back to
> four. It could one day jounce over to a snake eye and
> bring in a new ice age![2]

Or indeed to a six and to what has been called hothouse earth.

1

THE CAUSES OF CLIMATIC CHANGE

Why, then, does the climate change? And what is its time scale? There is no short, complete, or even adequate answer to either question, and most of the ideas which have been put forward remain controversial. For the sake of clarity climatic events can be put into three interlocking categories: those arising from events outside the earth; those generated within the terrestrial system; and those caused by man himself. All can deeply affect our lives; and each, however long-term and apparently farfetched, deserves consideration.

In the last resort, all major change must come as a result of the earth's relationship with the sun, that nuclear power station 93 million miles away. Any interference with the energy supply across space, any change in the way that energy is received on earth, and any change in the supply system itself would clearly have immediate and substantial effects. Here, then, is the first place to look for the causes of the major changes represented by the successive ice ages during the last 1,000 million years. Analysis of their timing suggests an approximate periodicity of some 150 million years between them with one apparent gap. A tentative explanation recently put forward by McCrea[3] and Williams[4] is that as the solar system rotates as part of the giant rotation of our galaxy over 300 or more million years, it twice encounters areas of dust in the spiral arms, and this dust inevitably affects the solar radiation reaching the earth. (This is not the occasion to describe the physical models constructed by McCrae and

Williams, but they are at present the subject of debate.) According to McCrae, the earth is now emerging from the spiral arm in Orion, and we are generally set fair for warmer conditions.

Moving from millions to thousands of years, and from interference with the energy supply to its receipt on earth, we come to the three variations in the earth's position with respect to the sun, known collectively as the Milankovitch effect. The amount of solar radiation reaching the earth varies according to the slight eccentricity of the earth's orbit, sometimes almost circular, sometimes elliptical, in an oscillation of between 90,000 and 100,000 years. When the orbit is most elliptical, the intensity of solar radiation can vary by up to 30% in the course of a year (at present it is around 7%). Another variation arises from the shifting tilt of the earth's axis of rotation in relation to the plane of its orbit in an oscillation of 40,000 years. The greater the tilt, the more the difference between summer and winter (the last maximum was 10,000 years ago). Finally there is a variation, this time of 21,000 years, in the wobble of the earth around its axis—the so-called precession of the equinoxes—and this determines the time at which the northern or southern hemisphere is closest to the sun (at present it is the largely oceanic southern hemisphere).

Much work has been done to assess the effects of these three major variations, and although few would claim that the relationship between them could alone cause the alternation between glacial and warm conditions in the last 1½ million years (if it were the sole cause, this oscillation would be permanent rather than—as is the case—exceptional), most are agreed that it has been a major factor. Tables have been made which show that the predicted variations in sunshine reaching a given point on the earth's surface during the last 700,000 years can be correlated with the actual changes of temperature recorded in isotopic analysis of certain marine fossils.[5] Certainly we must reckon with the Milankovitch effect in calculating our longer term future.[6]

Of more importance in the short term is the possibility of variation in solar radiation itself. Acceptance of the idea that the emission of energy from the sun is not perfectly regular, and that the so-called solar constant might turn out to be inconstant, is relatively new. A number of solar cycles have been suggested, ranging from 90 years to 27 days (the period of its rotation on its own axis), but the sunspot cycle of 11, or more accurately 22 years, is most famous. The connection between sunspots and the weather on earth used to be regarded as an old wives' tale, but recent research shows that it may well not be, although vital information is lacking and the mechanism is not yet understood.[7] Is it, for example, a coincidence that between 1645 and 1715, the period of "the Little Ice Age," sunspots became a fascinating rarity to astronomers, the display of solar activity in the upper atmosphere known as aurora (borealis or australis) was greatly reduced, and the dramatic jets and streamers, or coronae, usually seen around the sun at the time of an eclipse went unreported?

Sunspots are, of course, no more than a sign of magnetic activity in the sun, but their presence or absence could well indicate crucial variations in radiation. Lack of sunspots in 1976—the low point in the 22-year cycle—has already been blamed for current droughts in temperate parts of the northern hemisphere. Whatever may be happening now, it has been estimated that during the period 1645 to 1715 radiation could have been about 1.4 per cent lower than at present, a figure not inconsistent with what we can assess were average prevailing temperatures in the northern hemisphere at that time (about 1° to 2°C. less than at present). There is also evidence to suggest that the intensity of solar radiation increased around 1916.[8]

Our knowledge of the behavior of the sun has anyway been shaken by the failure over three years of experiments to find the predicted numbers of the changeless, massless particles known as neutrinos in the spectrum of solar radiation. Either the experiments were badly done, or our thinking about the nuclear processes at work in the sun will require radical revision. The very recent discovery that the sun is mysteriously pulsating at a rate of every 2 hours 40 minutes suggests that revision will be required. One of the highest scientific priorities is more precise measurement (to within 0.1% accuracy) of solar radiation over a period of years. Without it we can do little more than speculate about what could be one of the crucial factors in variations of the earth's climate.[9]

Two other external factors should be mentioned. The differential rotation of the planets, including the earth, has tidal effects on the surface of the sun, and the disturbances thus created almost certainly affect the earth at a rhythm of about 1,700 years. The pull of sun and moon, which creates the familiar ocean tides, also affects the atmosphere. Exceptionally high tides at intervals of about 1,800 years can change weather patterns by setting processes in train which take long to correct themselves: for example, the tidal maximum in high latitudes in 1433 may have contributed to the southward drift of Arctic pack ice, which in turn contributed to "the Little Ice Age."[10] There are other lesser factors. But those cited are enough to show the total dependence of the earth and its climate on the powerhouse of the sun, and sensitivity to the least variation in supply of energy or other activity upon it.

Of natural changes to the climate arising from within the terrestrial system, by far the most important are caused by the slow movement of the various pieces of the earth's crust —the so-called tectonic plates—in relation to each other. The drift of continents, and the rise and subsequent erosion of mountains along the plate boundaries, both at speeds rarely exceeding two or three centimeters a year, determine how the energy arriving from the sun is distributed within the earth's atmosphere. The discovery of fossilized tropical plants in Antarctica, of scratches left by glaciers in Brazil, or of seashells high in the Alps is less amazing when we think of the earth's crust as a cracked and bulging plastic cover subject to

varying pressures from inside. Changes up, down, or side-
ways of two centimeters a year may not seem relevant to
modern problems, or at most of interest only to scientists.
But they are crucial to our understanding of why the climate
should be as it is, and provide an important part of the explanation for the most recent as well as earlier ice ages.

The presence of land or landlocked sea at the poles seems
indispensable for the growth of the glaciers which make up
the present ice caps. Perennial ice now covers 11% of the
earth's land surface, and 7% of its seas. The drift of the Antarctic continent to its present isolated position, and the subsequent partial enclosure of the Arctic Ocean from most of
the warm currents moving north from the equator, helped
the slow accretion of ice sheets. Without these permanent
glaciers (those in Antarctica are probably more than 20 million years old), the processes which led to the successive ad-
vances and retreats of the ice in the last one and a half million
years could probably have never got started. Thus a particular configuration of land, sea, and ice is the stage on which all
climate is set. If the Gulf Stream were to alter its north-east-
erly flow a little to the south, as it did 18,000 years ago, the
British Isles and Western Europe could again have the climate
of the Hudson Bay in Canada on the same line of latitude.

The ice caps themselves occupy a vital role in the world
weather system, profoundly affecting ocean currents and
winds, and the transfer of heat between them. The East Antarctic and Greenland Sheets, both grounded on land above
sea level, are its anchors. By contrast, the West Antarctic
Sheet and most of the Arctic Sheet are unstable, and sensitive
to relatively small changes in air and ocean temperature. Ice
can anyway generate its own climate in the process known as
positive feedback. Once established—and that can be fast or
slow—snow and ice reflect the bulk of the sun's radiation
back into space. This creates colder weather, which in turn
leads to the extension of the snow and ice cover. This self-
reinforcing process can eventually reach stability, correct
itself, or go into reverse, when lack of evaporation from the

snow and ice over a large area reduces the quantity of precipitation in the form of new snow. Wind-blown dust from elsewhere can also reduce the reflectivity (or albedo) of the snow surface, and affect the process described above.

Several theories to explain the apparent rhythm of ice ages have been built on the interaction of ice and ocean current and wind. Most agree that there is an imbalance in the energy budget of ocean and atmosphere which causes an oscillation over tens of thousands of years between a warm mode and a cold mode. For present purposes it is enough to say that each is unstable. In the warm mode the shrinking of the ice caps brings warm water further towards the poles and a rise in sea level. Evaporation increases and with it the amount of precipitation. At the same time water cooled at the poles moves towards the equator. But increased snow at the poles and cooler water in temperate latitudes switches the world over to the cold mode. The ice sheets grow, sea levels drop, and temperatures fall in middle latitudes. Eventually this too corrects itself. The warm mode is resumed when the supply of snow fuelling the ice caps falls with decreased evaporation, and when the surface water, warmed by the sun, is no longer sufficiently cooled by contact with the ice (itself now extended into warmer latitudes) to have cooling effects elsewhere.

Another, now less popular, idea is that periodically vast quantities of West Antarctic ice become unstable and surge out to sea, lowering temperatures further north, increasing storminess, and eventually causing greater precipitation at the poles. Certainly the state of the polar ice sheets, and the drift of ice north and south from them, is a critical factor in determining the weather as well as the climate throughout the world.[11]

The process of positive feedback does not apply only to ice. Deserts also reflect back more heat than they receive, and can, if recent evidence is correct, both draw in and chill the air over them. Precipitation from outside, such as it is, is reduced, and the desert can thus extend itself. Other examples abound. One is the way in which a change in the temperature of the ocean surface can alter the quantity of heat absorbed by the air, which in turn causes changes in the atmosphere, which in turn enhance the change in the temperature of the ocean. The importance of the mechanism is that it gives relatively fast and prolonged momentum to what might otherwise seem slow and minor elements in climatic change. Even something ephemeral, including certain of the works of mankind, could press the button, and set in train a process which might not correct itself for thousands of years.

In this respect there has been much recent discussion of the role of volcanic emissions in the atmosphere. Volcanoes, most of which are along the boundaries of tectonic plates, blast immense quantities of matter into the sky during eruptions. Carbon dioxide, sulphur, and water vapor from this source have little climatic significance. But dust, which is rapidly blown high and wide, casts a veil over the atmosphere, and, depending on the size, color, and shape of the particles, shuts out more solar radiation from outside than it shuts in terrestrial radiation from below. The result is usually a general cooling effect at the surface.[12]

According to observations made at Manna Loa in Hawaii, the eruption of Mount Agung in Bali in 1963 led to a sharp decrease of nearly 2% in direct solar radiation. In spite of some countervailing effects, eruptions seem to be accompanied by wetter weather generally and storminess in temperate latitudes. Such effects can last anywhere from two to fifteen years, and in the event of successive eruptions much longer. Conceivably this could be one of the buttons which, if pressed, could set off the process of positive feedback. At present most authorities doubt it; but a good case has been made for linking the extent of volcanic activity with cooler periods in the immediate past. Bryson in particular attributes the cooling of the northern hemisphere since 1940 to an increase in the volume of particles of volcanic matter augmented by those of human origin.[13] Other types of dust, notably from deserts, are blown up into the atmosphere, and have effects similar to those of volcanic particles. In all, about a million tons fall to the earth's surface every year; but this should be compared with up to a 100 million tons which can fall after a major series of eruptions.[14]

Of the rhythms of wind and sea in changing climate in temporary or more permanent fashion, more is known of effects than causes. In the northern hemisphere some winds behave with fair regularity within the limits of the present system, but the circumpolar jet stream or vortex, blowing from west to east about six miles above the surface, is virtually a law unto itself. On its speed and strength, and on its zigzags over Europe, the Soviet Union, and North America, depend much of the weather in northern temperate latitudes and thus the harvests in the main grain growing areas of the world. If the jet stream moves north, it can suck up warm wet air after it from the south; if it moves south it can bring in cold dry air from the Arctic. No wonder that its swings and eddies are so carefully watched, particularly in the Soviet Union.[15] The same goes for the variations in the Asiatic monsoon. Another much slower natural variable is the apparent tendency of waves of weather to move westward at an almost constant rate of 0.6° of longitude a year, thus making the circuit of the world in just under six centuries.[16]

The variables in the sea are still less understood but more important for the weather system as a whole. We have already looked at the possibility of long oscillations creating and destroying parts of the polar ice caps. More than half the solar radiation reaching the surface of the earth is absorbed by the sea, largely in the top 300 feet. This acts as a giant reservoir of heat: some is evaporated into the atmosphere, some is moved and mixed downwards, and some is kept in the surface layer, and travels under the influence of the wind, differences in temperature and saltiness, and the rotation of the earth itself. The movement of currents and of huge slow eddies in the ocean (akin to storms in the atmosphere) have rhythms on time scales ranging from the length of a season to tens of thousands of years. They are of intimidating complexity but their influence on climate is in many cases decisive.[17]

One example will suffice. In normal circumstances a strong

Pacific current runs from the south northwards along and away from the coasts of Chile and Peru. This creates an up-welling of deep, cold water rich in nutrient salts, which nourishes the fish on which much of the Peruvian economy depends, and determines the local weather. Every now and again, roughly once in seven years, the current moves in-shore (a phenomenon known as El Niño) and the upwelling is blocked or diverted. This could follow from a weakening of the trade winds, and a shift in the eastbound mid-Pacific cur-rent. But, whatever the cause, the result is catastrophic for fish and men alike; and its repercussions go a long way, even pos-sibly as far as the other side of the Andes, where droughts coincided with the last appearance of El Niño in 1972. Like-wise, variations in the temperature of the Pacific as well as the Atlantic almost certainly affect the performance of the circumpolar jet stream, and thus the whole pattern of climate in the temperate part of the northern hemisphere. To them, as much as anything else, can we attribute unseasonal sunshine in Scotland, droughts in the Ukraine, and hurricanes in South Carolina.

With so many natural variables, each interacting with the other, how can we hope to understand, let alone predict, the behavior of the system as a whole? Most scientific work is done by reducing problems to manageable size in laboratories, but our only laboratory for climatic experiments is the earth itself. Although we have been able to observe and measure the effects of prolonged dust storms on the planet Mars and those of concentrations of carbon dioxide on the planet Venus, we have no means of trying out the effects of particu-lar climatic events—even if it were feasible—without our-selves being involved in, or rather subjected to, the conse-quences. This has particular importance when we turn to what man himself may now be doing to the climate.

We now enter an area of even greater uncertainty. On one point most people are agreed. By itself no human activity has—yet—altered or substantially affected the climate of the world as a whole. That is not to say that in combination with other factors human beings have not already contributed to, or possibly mitigated change. Nor that their activities have not had local or regional effects. Nor that before very long they could not set processes in train which could lead to minor fluctuations or conceivably major change. In some respects they may already be straining the tolerance of a system whose variable parts do not, as we have seen, need much to upset them. These variables comprise most of the elements in the heat balance: the myriad ways in which the earth's surface absorbs or reflects radiation from the sun; the amount of heat otherwise generated at the surface; and the contents of the earth's atmosphere with its load of dust, particles, and gaseous constituents (including the ozone layer in the stratosphere).

Human beings and their animals have been gnawing away at the surface of the earth for a long time. Something like 20% of the total area of the continents has been drastically changed.[18] The cutting down of trees for settlement and agriculture, the slash-and-burn method of cultivation in primitive societies, the proliferation of such grazing animals as goats and cattle, and the overuse and impoverishment of top soils have in the past affected the heat and water balance in specific areas. The amount of solar radiation absorbed by the grass, crop, or in some cases desert land which took the place of the ancient forests was less than before: the result was probably a cooler local climate and, depending on particular circumstances, less moisture evaporated and more water— when it came—was run off.[19] The inevitable increase of dust blowing up from the surface may have had local effects similar to those of volcanic eruptions or sandstorms.

For human beings the most important results of such changes were in the pattern of rainfall, and to a lesser extent temperature. For example, the progressive aridity in historical times of the swathe of land from the Mediterranean to northern India, once covered in dense forest and later the site of successive civilizations, seems to have been caused mostly by human destruction of the natural environment. Certainly most of the grain growing areas which supported large populations, including those of the Roman Empire, are now largely scrub or desert. According to recent calculations some 6.7% of the earth's surface - an area larger than Brazil - is man-made desert.[20] How much of all this can be attributed to the climatic results of the limited changes wrought by mankind is impossible to assess and a matter of definition. Apart from natural factors, there are many other man-made ones at work, including the destruction of the top soil.

In recent times two other man-made changes to the surface of the earth have become significant. The building of cities may not have affected the reflectivity of the earth as much as the substitution of grass, crop, or desert land for forest; but taking account of their concrete canyons and roads (roads now cover almost 1% of the United States)[21], and still more of the artificial energy generated within them, cities emit a good deal more heat than they receive: New York about six times more, Moscow three, and Sheffield one and a half.[22] They are notably warmer than the surrounding countryside, and cast a kind of heat shadow according to the direction of the prevailing wind. The global quantity of energy generated by mankind is only around .01% of that poured on top of the atmosphere by the sun. But these heat domes over urban areas undoubtedly change local climates. The warm air rises, increasing cloud and turbulence, which in turn increases rain and snowfall. But rain and snow rapidly disappear and surface humidity is relatively low. The results are complex and analysis of them is incomplete. But they range from the suggestion that Atlantic winter storms are attracted towards the heat dome over the urban concentration known in the trade as Bosnywash (Boston-New York-Washington) to the discovery that there is less rain and snow in cities (and downwind of them) at weekends when factory smoke and car exhausts are diminished.[23]

The second recent man-made change is the creation of artificial lakes and extended areas of irrigation, and the diversion of river systems. Irrigation is not of course new, and may have had minor climatic effects in the past (for example, the waterlogging and salinization of much of Mesopotamia contributed to its deterioration into desert and present climate). But the vast lakes and irrigation schemes of our own time are of a new order of magnitude: depending on the angle of the sun's rays, water retains and absorbs more heat than any land surface, and through evaporation adds vapor to the atmosphere. As a general rule, this should produce more cloud and higher rainfall downwind, but each case is of course particular to itself.

The diversion of rivers can have even greater effects. A good example - and worrisome case - is the proposal to divert the northward flowing rivers of Siberia to the arid lands of Central Asia. Whatever the beneficial effects in Central Asia, the loss of vast quantities of fresh water in the Arctic could affect the polar weather pattern: the salty sea water would freeze less readily and evaporation might increase, in turn increasing snowfall elsewhere. This in turn might affect the balance of permanent glacier and Arctic pack ice, and eventually modify the existing heat exchange between ocean and atmosphere, and of course the wind system in the northern hemisphere as a whole. Like such ideas as damming the Bering Straits or alteration in the flow of some of the Gulf Stream, the proposal to divert the Siberian rivers raises major international issues.

Perhaps the most obvious man-made change to the climate follows not from what people do to the surface of the earth but from what they deliberately put into the sky, an even bigger disposal unit than the sea. Since the beginning of the industrial revolution, the combustion of fossil fuels—coal, oil, and gas—has led to a steady increase in the quantity of carbon dioxide gas (CO_2) and aerosol particles in the atmosphere. Half or more of the increased supply of carbon dioxide finds its way into the sea or is absorbed by plants: but the remainder lingers in the air, and has risen from about 285 parts per million (ppm) in 1880 to 320 ppm in 1970, an increase of 10%. As the quantity is rising at an exponential rate, the next such increase could be in 20 years. Carbon dioxide blocks outgoing radiation from the earth more than incoming radiation from the sun, and thus has the so-called greenhouse effect.

How much the observed increase in carbon dioxide has in fact warmed the lower atmosphere is in dispute. Some calculations show that it should have warmed it by 0.2°C. to 0.3°C., but if so, other factors must have been operating the other way.[24] There is little dispute that a rise to 400 ppm should have clear effects, and other things being equal could raise average global temperatures, with greater or lesser regional variations, by 1°C. Such an increase would have perceptible consequences, particularly in the frontier areas between climatic zones; and 400 ppm would be by no means the limit if the consumption of fossil fuels continued to increase.

The quantity of man-made aerosol particles - industrial and chemically produced dust and smog - in the atmosphere has also increased. According to one authority, it now amounts to about 50 million tons annually and constitutes 10% to 20% of all atmospheric aerosols.[25] Here the primary effects are local. Most particles, like other forms of dust, are rained back on to the surface fairly soon, and do not spread far from the areas, usually the urban concentrations of the northern hemisphere, whence they came. Even so, by no means all return to the surface, and together they probably affect the radiation balance in the same fashion as carbon dioxide. With more industrialization their effects will obviously increase. What those effects are is still in dispute. The extent to which they absorb or reflect solar and terrestrial radiation depends on their size, color, and shape. But here even the best authorities can arrive at opposite conclusions. One believes that aerosol particles should recently have cooled the northern hemisphere by about 0.5°C., thus counteracting the rise in temperature caused by carbon dioxide;[26] while another does not rule out the possibility that they have recently had a warming effect at the surface in the same area.[27]

Nuclear explosions have long been under widespread popular suspicion for changing the climate or causing almost any apparent abnormality. In fact, so far as is known, their climatic consequences are not very different from those of volcanic eruptions. Whether the effects are local or general, short or relatively long-lived, depends on the size and altitude of the explosion, and thus the quantity of dust and other particles discharged into the atmosphere. Major explosions may also blow temporary holes in the ozone layer. But any cooling or increased storminess in the weather seem likely to be temporary, and no permanent climatic results of atmospheric nuclear testing have ever been shown.

Artificial weather modification has also been suspect. Here what has happened is much less important than what could happen. It is natural for people to want to modify the weather, and for thousands if not millions of years rainmakers have tried to work their magic. At least theoretically, it is now possible to induce rain, prevent hail, disperse fog, frustrate hurricanes, deluge enemies, and otherwise redirect the weather. So far, the seeding of clouds with dry ice or silver iodide has had only local results, generally below expectations. It is of course difficult to demonstrate cause and effect, and seeding has its believers and nonbelievers. But the potentialities for this as for other forms of weather modification have obvious international implications. One man's rain is another man's desert. Even the dispersal of a typhoon, which saves one area from destruction, means the denial of lifegiving water to another.

High in the gaseous envelope surrounding the earth is a wavy layer containing a small but vital quantity of the oxygen molecule O_3 or ozone (some .001%). Ozone is constantly created by the action of sunlight on normal oxygen molecules, and is as constantly destroyed after about 18 months through interaction with nitric oxide and other molecules rising from the earth. During that time it drifts from the equator towards the poles, where the ozone layer is at its thickest. Little is known about its behavior. But without ozone, life in its present form literally could not exist.

Its function is to absorb much of the ultraviolet radiation from the sun (in particular the wavelength of 0.26 millionths of a meter which would otherwise damage the DNA or reproductive molecule in all living systems). The variation in the thickness of the ozone layer is reflected in the ability of organisms, including the human species, to cope with different degrees of ultraviolet radiation. Thus white-skinned people who venture into the tropics or climb to high altitudes are more subject to sunburn and skin cancer than the brown or black-skinned inhabitants.

The ozone layer also determines the temperature of the stratosphere, and thus indirectly affects climatic conditions further down, through the differing rates at which it absorbs solar and terrestrial radiation. The role of the ozone layer in the history of the earth is unknown. But it has recently been suggested that substantial depletion of the ozone layer at the various times when the earth reversed its magnetic field could have contributed - to say no more - to the mass extinctions of animal life which have taken place at least eight times in the earth's history. The end of the dinosaurs some 65 million years ago is the best known.[28]

Anything which might damage the good health of the ozone layer is thus an immediate cause of concern; and in the last few years some alarming suggestions have been made about the effects of man-made pollutants upon it.[29] The most notorious are the chlorofluorocarbons (known commercially by a variety of names including freons), which are used as a propellant in spray or aerosol cans and as a refrigerant in cooling devices. Chlorofluorocarbons, once thought to be inert, rise slowly into the stratosphere, where they are turned by the actions of sunlight into fluorine and chlorine atoms, some of which (it is far from clear how many) in turn destroy ozone. The chemical oxides of nitrogen are less efficient but some again have a similar effect: here the most important are those (NO_x) injected into the stratosphere from the exhausts of high flying aircraft (especially supersonic transports), or from nuclear explosions, or from chemical processes on earth. Nor is this all. Other suspects are the nitrous oxide

(N_2O) produced in nitrogen fertilizer, brominated and chlorinated compounds used in the purification of drinking water and sewage, and carbon monoxide from car and other exhausts.

In spite of the massive work which has been done (notably by the Climatic Impact Assessment Program commissioned by the U.S. Department of Transportation), there is as yet little certitude about the effects of human activity on the ozone layer. With a normal fluctuation up to 15 per cent, the human contribution is hard to determine, but some models suggest that it is still less than 1 per cent. Again, it is more what could happen than what has happened which is alarming. Continuing increase in the manufacture of chlorofluorocarbons over the years or, as many would like to see, the multiplication many times of current production of nitrogen fertilizer, might eventually cause depletion of the ozone which is by any standards already significant.

What then? Most attention has so far been focused on the likely increase in the incidence of human skin cancer. But however unpleasant for the victims, this is less serious than the consequences for life as a whole. Experiments have shown that greatly increased exposure to ultraviolet radiation (more than would be likely from ozone depletion for a long time), slows up the growth of plants on land or in the sea, prevents in some cases the ripening of crops, accelerates genetic mutation, and damages the process of photosynthesis. Thus the bottom of the food chain might conceivably be affected.[30]

In this perspective, possible changes to the climate pale into insignificance. But changes there might well be. Ozone acts as a shutter for radiation in part of the infrared as well as the ultraviolet range of the solar spectrum, and variations in the thickness of the ozone layer may directly affect the climate.[31] Cooling or warming may depend on where the maximum concentration of ozone is: a decrease in altitude would tend to warm and an increase in altitude would tend to cool, but the effects of depletion on altitude are still unknown.

Better known but still in dispute is the result of increasing the quantity of chlorofluorocarbons, nitrogen oxides, and other chemicals in the atmosphere: here the effect would probably be similar to that of carbon dioxide, and if taken in isolation would cause some warming at the surface.

2

THE HUMAN RESPONSE
TO CHANGE

What conclusions can be drawn from this summary description of the processes of climatic change? Perhaps the first is to underline the fragmentary nature of our knowledge and the immense difficulty of assigning causes to effects. We can say on the basis of mathematical models that if such and such a factor could be isolated the result would be such and such. But in real life no factor can be so isolated, and there are many factors in this complex system of which we know little and there are probably others of which we know nothing.

Yet the second conclusion is surely that the attempt must be made. We have already greatly changed the environment of the earth, and every day that passes we change it more. Our actions are usually undertaken with local and short-term intent. Trees are felled, factories are built, cities spread out and up, heat is generated, to meet the particular needs of particular people at a particular point in time. By these means human society has grown in size and accomplishments like the accumulation of a coral reef around some tropical island. The builders of the reef worked to no plan and were largely unaware of each other's existence. So slow was the process that no one knew that they were changing the life of the shore, if not the island itself, by their actions. Yet the size and complexity of the structure, and the proliferation of creatures who came to live there could eventually threaten the conditions which first allowed its growth, and the ever changing sea could always strand or destroy it. We are more than coral reef builders or inhabitants. But the cumulative effects of our actions are so great that we too could damage the condition of our continued growth. To some extent we have the power to control and direct it. But we have to know what we are doing, and of course we also could be stranded or destroyed by changes in conditions from without.

The biggest threat we face is our own success as a species. Like other animals who have well adapted themselves to their environment, we have greatly increased in numbers, rising steeply from the beginning of the industrial revolution to an estimated 2,000 million in 1930 to around 4,000 million in 1975. The annual increase in 1930 was about 1.1 per cent. In 1975 it was around 2 per cent and could still be rising. Yet unlike most other animals we have contrived to remove most of the checks and balances which in the past kept us in our natural place. We have learned how to live in virtually every climate; we have changed the face of the continents to meet our needs; we face no serious challenge from other species, and know how to cope with most of the dangerous viruses and bacteria; we have changed the balance, number and genetic inheritance of animals and plants for our own purposes; and we have a system of morality deriving from pack and tribal instincts which, in spite of habitual collective violence between human groups, has established a conscious community of mankind in which each has a certain sense of responsibility for all.

No one knows how long the present dizzy expansion of human numbers can continue before stability is reached or catastrophe takes place. The dilemma was well put by A. V. Hill:

> Some might [take] the purely biological view that if men will breed like rabbits they must be allowed to die like rabbits . . . most people will say No. But suppose it were certain now that the pressure of increasing population, uncontrolled by disease, would lead not only to widespread exhaustion of the soil and of other capital resources but also to continuing and increasing interna-

tional tension and disorder, making it hard for civilization to continue: Would the majority of humane and
reasonable people then change their minds? If ethical
principles deny our right to do evil in order that good
may come, are we justified in doing good when the fore-
seeable consequence is evil?[32]

For the moment the notion of expansion is deeply embed-
ded in our psychology. No country is immune from it. We
look to meet increasing demands for food or higher living
standards, and to rectify the lopsidedness of our present distribution of human wealth, by ever greater and more effec-
tive exploitation of natural resources, euphemistically described as development. Failure to develop or otherwise ex-
pand our economies has come to imply and perhaps to mean
stagnation, dislocation or even social breakdown. No responsible and, still less, elected government could lightly sac-
rifice a short-term and direct advantage in terms of wealth
and employment for its people to avoid a long-term, indirect
and uncertain disadvantage for the human race of life as a
whole. Even the idea that we could dangerously pollute our
environment has been described as a luxury of the rich; and
even in so rich a society as the United States, it may seem
more important to save jobs at Dupont than to risk depletion
of the ozone layer.

What place should climatic factors have in this depressing
equation? Perhaps the single most important one is that over-
population, with all that it implies, greatly diminishes our
ability to respond to change. We have seen that the climate is
changing or fluctuating all the time, and that very small
changes can have very big effects. In the past, people have
responded to change like any other animal. They have ex-
ploited the opportunities it provided; or they have moved
elsewhere; or they have adapted themselves and made the
best of it. Thus during the last glaciation men were able to
move across the land bridge of what is now the Bering Straits
to spread across the Americas in perhaps the greatest of population explosions before our own time. Desert droughts in

the Sahara pushed populations southwards, or led to special adaptations like those of the Bedouin, or the Bushmen of the Kalahari. Warmer conditions in Greenland attracted farmers in the 11th century but they were gone by the 15th when the cold returned.

By contrast, change now and still more in the future could cause havoc, especially along the boundaries of the climatic zones. Some would certainly benefit from the kind of minor fluctuations we have seen since the ice retreated 10,000 to 11,000 years ago. But for most, change could only be for the worse. It was no longer possible for people to respond to the droughts of the early 1970s with their feet. There were other people and their frontiers in the way. Indeed nowhere in the world are there any open frontiers left. As for adaptation to new and perhaps less favorable conditions, many things can be done if people will do them and the necessary skills can be acquired.[33] But there are clear limits, and these are everywhere in sight. This decline in flexibility of response implies a new and alarming vulnerability to climatic change from any quarter, whether from outside the earth, from the processes at work within it, from the activities of mankind, or from all three.

In these circumstances it is worth looking at some of the possible consequences of climatic change. Both the range of possibilities and the time scale in which change could take place are vast. But we should be wrong to think that movement to one or other end of the range (assuming we are somewhere in the middle) would necessarily take a long time. Both drastic cooling and drastic warming could take place relatively quickly. To judge from our inevitably fragmentary knowledge of what happened 90,000 years ago, glaciation could begin in less than a century; and further warming could begin even faster. In any case, much less than drastic change could, as we have seen, affect millions of people in one season, let alone a year or tens of years.

For some time most observers ready to chance an opinion have predicted a cooling trend, and some have gone so far as to suggest that we are gradually moving back into an ice age. The evidence for this is partly statistical. Many aspects of the glacial fluctuations of the last 700,000 years can be interpreted in terms of a 100,000 year cycle, beginning with warm conditions similar to or warmer than our own. There has been a gradual cooling, culminating in a short intensely cold period, followed by a sudden return to warm conditions.[34] Such warm periods, themselves abnormal in the sense that they have prevailed for only 10 per cent of the last million years, have lasted around 10,000 years each. On this reckoning our time should soon be up, and if the climate were governed by insurance calculations, we should already be taking out policies to protect ourselves. We have already looked at some of the possible reasons for this cycle. There is the particular orbit, tilt, and wobble of the earth: the combination of these factors may not be dissimilar from that which prevailed 90,000 years ago. According to calculations made by Calder on the basis of variation in sunshine at latitude 50° North, the trend is clearly towards glacial conditions.[35] Then there is the evidence for slow oscillation within the oceans which seems to be moving into the cold mode. Those ephemeral changes, such as an increase in volcanic dust and man-made particles, could also be having an effect, and were called in aid to explain the cooling trend between 1945 and 1970. But no evidence is conclusive, and the shape of trends is different on different time scales.

The precise effects of cooling, fast or slow, are likewise unknown, but we can make some guesses from what happened on previous occasions. The onset of a major glaciation would in broad terms shift the present boundaries between climatic zones southwards in the northern hemisphere and northwards in the southern one. Each year the cover of snow and ice on land in the northern hemisphere would last longer or not melt at all. Growing seasons would become steadily shorter, and yields from most of the present grain growing areas of the world would sharply decline. It was once supposed that in such conditions there would be greater rainfall in the tropics, but this is not necessarily the case. Indeed, drought might come to areas now relatively free of it. The absorption of vast quantities of water into the spreading ice caps would lower sea levels worldwide, exposing much of the present continental shelves, changing the pattern of evaporation, and the direction of some winds and currents.

Obviously, the redevelopment of a glacier in the English Channel, the evolution of tundra conditions in the Great Plains, or the disappearance of New Zealand under ice would depend on particular temperatures and the extent of glaciation round the poles. But if anything like the last glaciation took place, we could say that most of Northern Europe north of the line of the English Channel, a substantial part of North America and the Soviet Union, most of the mountain countries of the world, and parts of China and Australasia would be buried under ice hundreds if not thousands of feet thick. The pattern would not be consistent. In some areas there might be little change. Differences in temperature and precipitation between one zone and another would be greater than they are now. Ocean temperatures in the tropics might even be warmer. But the world as we know it would have become unrecognizable, and its carrying capacity for life, including that of man, would be drastically altered. There could of course be many gradations, ranging from conditions still colder than our world has known before, to the 1°C. drop in the average temperature of the northern hemisphere, which prevailed during "the Little Ice Age" of the 17th century.

But what now of movement the other way towards a warmer earth? In a perspective of millions of years a climate considerably warmer than the present is normal. It may be that we are now emerging from the cyclical glaciations of every 150 million years or so, as the solar system moves out of an area of galactic dust or the sun itself behaves in different fashion. Whether these extra-terrestrial influences will bring back the apparently warm and steady conditions of earlier epochs is highly speculative. But there are other factors of much shorter time scale to suggest warming up. These are the work of mankind itself. We have already seen the changes made to the surface of the earth, the development of heat domes over cities, and the injection of increasing quantities of carbon dioxide, dust, and other particles into the atmosphere. Of most significance for the future are the likely increase in carbon dioxide (the state of the carbon dioxide atmosphere of the planet Venus at 450°C. represents an awful warning); and the likely increase in energy generated or captured on the surface of the earth.

The global amount of energy generated by man is, as remarked above, no more than .01 per cent of that poured on top of the atmosphere by the sun. But however tiny now, this proportion is rising fast, and greater production of energy is regarded by every government in the world not just as desirable but as indispensable if more people are to be fed and living standards are to be raised. Even if the quantity of energy generated by combustion of fossil fuels with its fallout of carbon dioxide will eventually decline as supplies of oil, gas, and coal run out, other substantial sources of energy are already available or in prospect: nuclear fission and probably fusion, geothermal, solar, and tidal power among others. In this field more than in most, there are unlikely to be technical problems which human ingenuity cannot overcome. The curve of demand appears ever upwards, even in the United States where more energy is consumed than in the rest of the world put together. On the basis that generation of energy to meet demand continues to rise at its present rate, it has been calculated that the human addition to the energy received at the top of the atmosphere from the sun would rise to around .1 per cent by 2015 to 2035, 1 per cent by 2055 to 2095, 10 per cent by 2095 to 2155 and 100 per cent by 2135 to 2215.[36]

These figures may be unrealistic, but they seem to point up a trend. According to the Soviet meteorologist Budyko, a rise to only 1 per cent would be sufficient to melt the ice caps.

That could be a century away on these calculations, but
before then major distortions in the climate would have
become evident. Global effects are no more than the aggre-
gate of local effects, and we have already seen that heat
domes over urban conglomerations are affecting local climates. As cities increase in size to accommodate the rising
population, and more and more energy is generated in or
around them to meet human needs, the extent and temperature of the heat domes will increase with local, regional, and
eventually global consequences. How big those consequences
are will of course depend on a multiplicity of other factors.

Again we can only guess at the global effects of a general
warming, and again there could be many gradations. The
frontiers of the present climatic zones would probably shift
northwards in the northern hemisphere and southwards in
the southern one, but the pattern would be confused by such
factors as the distribution of heat domes. The critical point
would be reached when substantial quantities of polar ice
began to melt. The detachment of icebergs and their drift
towards more temperate seas, and the concentration of ocean
currents nearer or round the poles would initially have cooling effects in middle latitudes. But on the assumption that the
warming continued and there was no switch back to a cold
mode, the polar ice would eventually slide off or melt on the
land masses underlying the Antarctic and part of the Arctic
ice caps, and world sea levels would rise dramatically. It has
been calculated that the melting of the grounded ice in West
Antarctica alone would raise sea levels by about 15 feet; and
if the rest of the Antarctic cap and that over Greenland followed, levels would rise by another 185 feet. A glance at a
contour map shows that if the sea rose by 200 feet the face of
the continents would change as radically as in a renewed
glaciation. Most of the world's great cities and much of the
agricultural land would disappear beneath the water. And
this would be only one of the consequences for the surface of
the earth and its climate.

So much for the two extremes, neither of them less plausible nor likely for being an extreme. They help us to realize how much we are the creatures of our present balance between them, and how disrupting a major tilt in either direction would be. Each hypothesis naturally leaves out the factors which support the other, and their synthesis remains out of reach of human calculation. The further we look the more we find missing from our equations; and even if we fully understood the natural rhythm, including the behavior of the sun, the oscillations of ice, current, and wind, and the innumerable mechanisms of heat exchange over land and sea, we would still be unable to predict the future from the past. For the activities of our own species have in this as in so many other fields produced new factors which make the past a most uncertain guide.

More specifically, we cannot now exclude the thought that in the future a natural trend towards renewed glaciation might be mitigated or stopped by mankind itself. Eventually this could be by deliberate act. We can even imagine the institution of a kind of international thermostat for the management of the world's climate. We may be sure it would be designed to maintain the status quo.

For most people the best that can be done is to work in the hope and on the assumption that something like the present climate will continue indefinitely. Drastic cooling or drastic warming look like science fiction, and even fluctuations, being unpredictable, have been excluded from individual, national or international planning. In the memories of the majority the climate has not changed often or drastically enough to bring about worse than local or temporary disasters. Thus the swings of current climate, seasonal or otherwise, have come to be seen as the extremes of variability, and on that basis land and resources have been occupied, cultivated, and developed to the natural limit. For the minority along the boundaries between climatic zones the hazards have always been greater, and people have adapted themselves accordingly. But even their memories are short. One of the reasons for the extent of the disaster in the Sahel in the early 1970s was that the nomadic inhabitants, encouraged by so-called experts from outside, had begun to settle down, and had increased not only their own numbers but those of their herds of cattle and goats far beyond the grazing capacity of the land in other than optimum circumstances. The effects of a periodic drought were thus multiplied into a natural as well as human catastrophe.[37]

It may be understandable that climates should seem to last forever, but if this assumption did little harm in the past it could do a lot now or in the future. An assumption of stability invites planning for the optimum, and planning for the optimum leads to maximum exploitation of land and other resources. Any man-made system, whether a machine, a bridge, or a farm, tends towards the optimum, and the optimum tends to exclude the apparently unnecessary or redundant. Provided that stability is maintained, the system should work with increasing efficiency as improvements are constantly made to it. The same goes for the adaptation of an animal species to its environment. But the moment the environment changes, those who are best adapted to it suffer most and have the greatest difficulty in adjusting themselves. Without tolerance in its working parts the machine cannot withstand shock; without some measure of engineering redundancy, the bridge collapses under stress; and without flexibility in land use and genetic variability in crops, the farm is ruined by prolonged rain or drought. If excessive reliance on the optimum was the lesson of the Sahel in 1972, it could be the lesson elsewhere in the future as governments seek with all the apparatus of technology to produce greater and greater yields under the relentless pressure of increasing population.

This is not the occasion to reopen the controversy over the balance of population increase and food supply initiated by Malthus in his famous *Essay on the Principle of Population* in 1798. It is enough to say here that maximum exploitation of land and other resources for the production of food can prove hazardous if not dangerous to present as well as future generations if it is based on the notion of a stable environment and ignores the climatic dimension. The variability of the climate requires a corresponding variability in those who live in it, whether animal or plant; and all future planning, all development of skills for increasing food supplies and raising living standards, must take account of the possibility of drastic change and the certainty of continuing fluctuations, and thus be so far as possible geared to the worst rather than the best in prevailing circumstances.

The need for such an approach has been well illustrated in the last five years. The warmth of the first part of the century and even the slight cooling of the 1950s produced generally favorable conditions for agriculture. More recently, increased food production has played an important part in the boom conditions of the world economy as a whole. It was a time when miracle grains were first introduced, and many then thought that the green revolution would turn out to be as important as the industrial one in extending and improving the human condition. A succession of shocks came in the 1970s which invalidated many assumptions. 1972 was almost universally bad. Cold spread southwards from the north pole; and record low temperatures were reported in Greenland and the East Canadian Arctic; and the pack ice drifted well into temperate latitudes. Changes in the route of the circumpolar vortex caused the worst drought in the Moscow area for many centuries and excessive rain in the grain growing areas of the United States and Canada. Along the boundaries of the tropics a swathe of droughts went round the world, affecting sub-Sahara Africa (including the Sahel), India and South East Asia, parts of China and Australia, and Central and South America (where El Niño took the Humboldt current out to sea). In 1973 conditions were generally better with some bad spots, particularly in Asia. But 1974 was another bad year with results similar to those of 1972, and the prevailing energy crisis made things worse. We have yet to evaluate the outcome of 1976.

These disruptions had global effects. Food production,

which had been rising by 3.1 per cent a year between 1952 and 1962, and by 2.7 per cent a year between 1962 and 1972, actually dropped by 1 per cent in 1972. Grain resources fell drastically, markets were disrupted and prices rose. The severity of local disasters was somewhat mitigated, or at least obscured, by great improvement in the world system for the distribution of food, but by 1975 the ability of governments to respond to another such crisis was much reduced. Expressed as days of annual grain consumption (a somewhat uncertain measurement, but good enough as a general indication) reserves fell from 105 days in 1961 to 89 in 1970 to 55 in 1973 to 35 in 1975 to an estimated 31 in 1976.[38]

The crisis seemed to bring out certain trends of which most people until then had been unaware. The whole pattern of the world grain trade was undergoing change. In the period 1934 to 1938 the only substantial importer of grain was Western Europe. Other parts of the world were self-sufficient or net exporters. By 1973-1974 the picture was quite different, and according to preliminary estimates it has changed more since.[39] Today the only substantial exporter is North America, and with the exception of Australia and New Zealand, which have increased their exports over the last ten years, the other main regions—Asia, Africa, the Soviet Union, Eastern Europe, Western Europe, and Latin America—are net importers. It should be added that within this pattern much of North American grain exports to Western Europe and Japan are now animal feeds, a token of higher living standards in those countries. For others the import of North American grains, above all in bad years, has become a factor of major importance in keeping growing populations alive.

The energy crisis of 1974 brought out another vital point. It revealed how dependent increased food production, in particular that from miracle grains, was upon the supply of nitrogen fertilizer. Natural gas is a major element in the manufacture, and energy a major cost. The areas where the use of fertilizer would have the best result (in short, those areas where it has so far been relatively little used) are those which could least afford higher prices. The same goes for many pesticides.

It was also about this time that other limitations on increasing food production became more widely recognized. This is not the place for listing them or considering how and whether they can be overcome, but the main ones should be mentioned. Although much land in the world, including forest, could theoretically be ploughed up or otherwise used for human purposes, the hazards are much greater than most people once supposed. We have already glanced at the results of over-grazing in the Sahel. Another equally painful example is to be found in the consequences of destruction of tropical rain forest. Exposure of the underlying soils to high temperatures and heavy rainfall can cause them to form a brick-like compound called laterite. This virtually rules out agriculture and can turn the area into desert, with obvious climatic implications. This has happened in many places between latitudes 30° South and 30° North, and shows the extent to which tropical rain forest should be left as it is.[40]

Then there are the limitations on miracle grains. Properly used with abundant fertilizer and water they live up to their name, and could be more widely used than they are. But they are less adaptable than natural species and thus more vulnerable to change; and whatever the ingenuity of the genetic engineers, their yield has a maximum like everything else. There is also the problem of water. Apart from the vagaries of rainfall, the amount of extra water which can be obtained from river diversion, desalinization, or extraction from underground sources (in many cases not replaced) is obviously limited, and is anyway needed for more purposes than agriculture. Lack of water is likely to be an increasing constraint on industrial as well as agricultural development. As for the food resources of the sea, which were once thought to be limitless, the world fish catch has been down and up since 1970, partly as a result of over-exploitation, and possibly also because of pollution of certain vital areas.

Thus, by the middle of this decade it was clear to those who wished to see how vulnerable human food supplies had become: grain reserves were dangerously low after two bad years; there was increasing world dependence on one grain-growing area; the prospects for a significant increase in the quantity of land under cultivation was at best uncertain; the success of new agrarian methods had its limitations, financial and otherwise; water was in short supply for agricultural purposes; and even the sea—the source of life itself—was not a bottomless resource. Yet in 1972, 1973 and 1974 alone, the world population rose by about 240 million people, more than the present population of the United States.

In such circumstances it is difficult to be optimistic about our ability to cope with the consequences of the next "bad" year or set of "bad" years, or more objectively, the next small fluctuation in a continuously fluctuating climate. This is only one aspect of the problem created by increasing population and demand for higher living standards, but it could prove to be decisive. Little imagination is needed to work out some of the consequences. They range from increasing social disruption within communities to war between them over such age-old issues as fertile land and water supplies, the deepening division between rich and poor in favored and unfavored parts of the world, the development of new patterns of political dominance, and, perhaps worst for our species as a whole, the fouling of the future for the sake of survival in the present.[41] For as we have seen, the climate itself could be put at risk by the activities, deliberate or inadvertent, of mankind, and there will be increasing temptation for governments, under pressure from the hungry, the deprived, or the unemployed, to take actions which not only beggar their neighbors, but also damage or alter the delicate mechanisms of the atmosphere.

None of these horrendous things may happen. We may eventually achieve a balance in our affairs and a limit to our population with no more than local disruptions and disasters to which we are—or should be—accustomed. In any case there is much that we could do if we had the will to do it. The remainder of this book is devoted to consideration of what is being done and what could be done within the climatic dimension.

3
A CALL FOR
ACTION

It should go without saying that we are all in this together. The boundaries between us on the surface can no more stretch into the space through which we move at 20 miles a second than penetrate the earth's slowly turning metallic core. Ideally, all work on the climate should be done or coordinated under international auspices, and any decisions which governments singly or together may take in that respect should have the sanction of the world community. This may not always be possible. Difficult political and economic issues are often involved. But it should remain the aim, in spite of the somewhat discouraging history of such common endeavors. If they are urgent, they tend to lose responsibility to individual governments; and if they are long-term, they tend to run out of money and support. Climatic problems are at once important, urgent, and long-term.

There are four main areas in which action is required: 1) the accumulation and dissemination of greater knowledge about the climate; 2) international agreement on how to avoid activities which might by affecting the climate do prejudice to others, and on how to cope with climatic crises in the future; 3) the creation of institutions to exercise responsibility for the agreements reached; and 4) international agreement to prevent the modification of the climate for purposes of war. Each is now examined in turn.

(1) Accumulation and dissemination of greater knowledge about the climate.

Nearly everyone who has worked on climatic problems begins and ends by bewailing the lack of firm scientific information about them. It is almost a convention that books, reports, and articles on the subject conclude with recommendations for yet further study, yet wider observations, and yet better coordinated action. This book is no exception.

Yet a good start has already been made. The World Meteorological Organization long provided a general institutional umbrella. Precedents for practical international cooperation in the field were set in the 1950s by such events as the International Geophysical Year. In the following decade greater interest in both short-term weather forecasting and the behavior of the climate as a whole led to a joint recommendation from the World Meteorological Organization and the International Council of Scientific Unions for the creation of a Global Atmospheric Research Program (hereafter known as GARP) to accomplish the objectives stated in UN Resolutions 1721 (XVI) and 1802 (XVII):

> . . . to advance the state of atmospheric sciences and technology so as to provide greater knowledge of basic physical forces affecting climate . . .; to develop existing weather forecasting capabilities . . .; [and] to develop an expanded program of atmospheric science research which will complement the programs fostered by the World Meteorological Organization.

Since then work has proliferated on both the international and national level. It forms part of a still wider effort to increase our knowledge of the earth and its resources, including the sea. It is also part of the background to all discussion about the future of the world economy. More particularly, the Joint Organizing Committee of GARP and its subsidiary or associated organizations have sponsored work and conferences on such problems as the physical bases of climate and climatic modelling, the reconstruction of past climates, and long-term climatic fluctuations. In 1974 the first major GARP experiment took place, designed primarily to elucidate the behavior of the clouds of the tropical Atlantic; and in 1978 the first global GARP experiment will cover the world in an attempt to put together over a year precise information about the operation of the whole weather system, using for the purpose satellites, balloons, buoys, ships, aircraft, and the resources of the World Weather Watch chain of weather stations.

In some countries national GARP Committees have been set up, and regional studies have gone ahead. In 1972 the United States Committee for GARP appointed a Panel on Climatic Variation to study climatic problems, submit recommendations on what GARP objectives might be, and propose a national climatic research program. The result was the valuable report entitled *Understanding Climatic Change*, published by the National Academy of Sciences in 1975. This drew on work already done elsewhere, and incorporated earlier recommendations (including some made in reports from the Massachusetts Institute of Technology in 1970 and 1971).[42] Work in the United States on climatic problems is proceeding in universities, institutes, observatories, and laboratories around the country, and there is a National Center for Atmospheric Research in Colorado. In Britain the Climatic Research Institute at the University of East Anglia and the Meteorological Office have done pioneer work across the whole field. In the Soviet Union there has long been concentration on Arctic problems, and the Russians promoted the POLEX project, which is associated with Canadian and American work on Arctic ice dynamics. Many other countries have elaborate programs of their own. The list is too long to give here. While the bulk of the work is done nationally, the results are for the most part available to the world community as a whole.

These results are so far partial and meager. They serve to illuminate the extent of our ignorance. But at least we know pretty well what we are looking for and where information is most needed. It falls into three main categories: the working of the present system; the reasons for climatic change, including man-made effects; and the impact on human affairs. Within this framework people have their own special interests and order of priorities. High on nearly all of them are the global heat balance and exchange system between ocean and atmosphere, the role of the land surface, particularly deserts, and the behavior of ocean currents, ice and snow cover. Next come the solar constant and other extraterrestrial influences, the long oscillations of ocean and ice, the influence of dust, other particles and chemicals in the atmosphere, the effects of increased generation of energy, and the state of the ozone layer. The list concludes with the myriad consequences of change on human food, water and energy supplies, and finally, the structure of human society itself.

With so much work in hand, it may seem unnecessary to draw attention to one somewhat political requirement. It is for all governments to provide full and honest information about climatic events in regions under their control, and to do so according to international standards. At present the record is patchy. Some governments lack the means and experience to gather such information themselves and are reluctant to admit observers from outside. Moreover, their statistical methods are antique. Others withhold information for commercial reasons or plead the requirements of national security. In some respects the resulting gaps can be filled from information from meteorological and other satellites, but this is inevitably incomplete. For small countries it may not matter. But in the case of China, whose statistics are suspect, and the Soviet Union, for whom secrecy is a disease, lack of reliable and full information is seriously damaging. Even efforts to persuade the Russians in their own interest to provide information on crop prospects to avoid subsequent disruption of world grain markets have been unavailing. The problem could arise in acute form if the idea of regular climatic censuses is pursued, or if, as seems sensible, there is increasing international division of labor in the various fields of climatic research. In the future, information will increasingly be needed in areas not hitherto subject to international scrutiny. The effects of urban, industrial, and even agricultural pollution provide an obvious example. Many governments will be reluctant to oblige until they feel their countries damaged by the activities of others.

(2) International agreement on how to avoid activities which might by affecting the climate do damage to others and on how to cope with climatic crises in the future.

The principle is so obvious that no international agreement might seem necessary. But the problem is less simple than it looks. We have already seen the possible consequences of a scheme which, although it might make parts of Central Asia blossom like the rose, would risk affecting a part of the world's climate at one of its most critical points in the Arctic Ocean. On a smaller scale, seeding of the clouds to induce rain in one place could prevent it from falling in another where it is equally needed. This may already have happened in Israel at the expense of Syria, Lebanon, and parts of Jordan.[43] Arguments between governors of states in the United States indicate that it may have happened there too. The list of possible actions of this kind is already long and getting longer.

In nearly all such cases a major difficulty is our inability in current terms to prove cause and effect conclusively. Nothing is clear-cut. Those who divert rivers or seed clouds can plausibly maintain that changes elsewhere would have happened anyway. Governments which had authorized such actions would naturally enjoy the support of those who had benefited from them, and would strongly resist pressure from outside to undo—if it were possible—what had been done, to make reparation, or to undertake not to repeat such operations. It is arguable that in the future, as populations and demands on resources continue to increase, governments will be under mounting domestic pressure to put national requirements first to ensure their own survival as well as that of their people.

If the world is not to relapse into anarchy, with states warring over use and abuse of natural resources, some sort of international agreement in this respect—a self-denying ordinance and commitment to consult—will be essential. Our increasing ability deliberately or inadvertently to alter the climate makes the need for such an agreement urgent. Several factors favor its early negotiation. Governments are becoming better aware of the unitary character of the atmosphere and the climate within it. Those who chose to alter it for short-term advantage could ultimately suffer as much as their neighbors. The Soviet Union does not want increased snowfall in the Arctic any more than do Canada or Greenland. Cause and effect may not always be certain, but as knowledge increases links can be better established. With increasing populations and corresponding efforts to make the most of existing climatic and other circumstances, governments are becoming more attached to and dependent on the maintenance of a broad status quo as a framework for economic development. Risks become greater as economies get nearer the margin and flexibility diminishes. In such circumstances every country becomes more vulnerable to the actions of others, and more aware of its own vulnerability to change: some to the movement of ice, some to variations in the circumpolar vortex, some to the spread of desert, and some to shifts in seasonal rainfall.

Negotiation of such an agreement would obviously be very difficult, and the results might fall far short of what is desirable. But it should at least be possible to establish a framework which could be strengthened and enlarged as circumstances later required. The agreement might fall into four parts.

The first would be designed to cover all major experiments by governments (or those for whom they were responsible) which were intended to test the behavior of the climate or might inadvertently do so. There would be obvious problems over the definition of what should count as a major experiment. One suggestion is that the criterion might be any experiment in persistent or long-term climatic modification "directly affecting over 1 million square kilometers," and that those in this category should be prevented until the scientific community had reached a consensus on the consequences.[44]

This scarcely goes far enough. Other experiments which should be covered are smaller-scale ones with large probable effects, and those not directly concerned with the climate but with probable climatic impact. In some cases it might be necessary to require their prohibition pending international approval, and in others to make mandatory arrangements for consultation before they took place.

Examples of activities which should fall into one or other of these categories are experiments in rainmaking and control of hailstorms over a defined area; attempts to disperse hurricanes and typhoons; putting certain objects into space (such as the needles placed in orbit by the United States several years ago in defiance of protests from much of the scientific community); towing Antarctic icebergs northwards to provide fresh water to arid regions; tapping geothermal power from the magma underlying the division between tectonic plates at the bottom of the sea; burning sulphur in the upper atmosphere to keep the world's temperature down; and experiments in diversion of ocean currents, or in bringing cold water from the bottom of the sea as an industrial coolant or as an additional supply of nutrient salts. Some such experiments might be of scientific value and economic benefit and deserve full international encouragement and support. The purpose of an agreement would not be to frustrate them, but simply to ensure that their implications were properly considered and understood in time.

The second part of the agreement would be more ambitious. It would be designed to cover all actions by governments (or those for whom they were responsible) which were intended to change global, regional, or local climates in temporary or permanent fashion, or might inadvertently do so. It would thus follow naturally from the first part of the agreement. Again there would be problems of definition. In the words of two Soviet scientists who favor the idea:

. . . Any international regulations which are elaborated must take into account the consequences [for] all

elements of the environment and the evaluation of bene-
fits to be expected as well as possible adverse effects of
the methods used.[45]

So the scope would necessarily be wide. Within it, it would
again be necessary to distinguish between activities to be pro-
hibited pending international approval and those subject to
mandatory arrangements for prior consultation.

Examples indicate the complexity and delicacy of the issues
which would be raised. Apart from deliberate attempts to
change the climate, they include the permanent diversion of
major rivers (as aready discussed above); the construction of
river dams and irrigation systems likely to affect an area of
given size (the unforeseen and multiple consequences of the
Aswan dam for the Eastern Mediterranean as well as the Nile
valley are a case in point); the permanent diversion of ocean
currents, blocking of such natural waterways as the Bering
Straits, and building of a direct canal (i.e., without locks)
between the Atlantic and the Pacific; efforts to melt parts of
the polar ice caps (one bright idea is to spray sea ice with millions of tons of soot); oil drilling in such areas as the Arctic
where major spills would have incalculable and possibly irreversible effects; any plans to bring about major change in the
surface of the earth in an area of given size (as in the current
deforestation of Brazil); and certain industrial activities
which at a given level of intensity are known to have appre-
ciable effects on the atmosphere and climate.

This brings us to the third part of the agreement. It seems
virtually certain that there will be many activities with the
power to affect the climate which governments would not
wish to see included. This is not necessarily or only due to
national egotism or pressure of short-term economic interests. It arises from the unplanned nature of human affairs,
the gradual evolution of economic processes which once
started are hard to stop, and the genuine difficulty of demon-
strating cause and effect. In these circumstances it might be as
well to recognize reality from the start, and rather than try to
dragoon governments into obligations which they might not

accept or might later ignore, work instead for international endorsement of a voluntary code of good climatic behavior.

In this way the agreement as a whole could be made more comprehensive; and as knowledge increased and dangers became more specific and evident, items in the third part could be moved into the second, and new ones could go into the third. Examples of what might now be included in the third part are care of agricultural and forest land so that changes do not adversely affect others (the recent floods in Bangladesh could well have been made more severe by deforestation in Nepal); the local effects of urban and industrial activity, including generation of energy; and the production of chemicals or use of the upper atmosphere by aircraft in such a way as to affect the ozone layer.

A fourth part of the agreement would be to make general provision for coping with climatic crises, natural or manmade, in the future and to fix the point of administrative responsibility for coordination of international action. Such responsibility might include identification, study, and prediction of possible hazards; the provisions of advice and technical assistance on what might or should be done; and the mobilization of resources to help countries particularly affected.

(3) The creation of institutions to exercise responsibility for the agreements reached.

As we have seen, there are already institutions enough (if not too many) for the receipt and dissemination of information and coordination of climatic research across the whole field. It might be possible to extend their responsibilities and build on what exists. But as rationalization will anyway be necessary sooner or later, the conclusion of a major international agreement would be the occasion for reorganization and creation of a new institution within the United Nations framework. This institution could take over the functions and responsibilities of all existing international organizations in the field, including GARP, and the present World Meteorological Organization would become subsidiary to it.

The new institution, which might be called the World Climatic and Meteorological Organization, would have two main functions in regard to the agreement. Both would be more easily performed if the institution would take over all existing organizations. The first would be to act as its custodian and take responsibility for the work arising out of it. If the agreement worked as it should, there would be continuing consultation on climatic issues within its framework, and periodic meetings and conferences to consider action on specific points raised by governments. It would, for example, be necessary for the institution to decide on the basis of the best scientific advice whether this or that experiment should be authorized; to rule on whether particular activities fell within the scope of the agreement, and were or were not justified; to hear complaints from one government about the activities of another and if necessary arbitrate between them; to cope as far as possible with the results of climatic crises as and when they arose, and generally fulfill the provisions of the fourth part of the agreement; and to make recommendations to governments on changes within the agreement (moving items from one part to another) and on how the agreement should be developed and if necessary enlarged to meet new requirements and changing world circumstances.

The second main function of the institution would be to see that the agreement and the decisions arising from it were fully respected and, where appropriate, enforced. This difficult problem would of course arise from the day that drafting of the agreement began. The choice for the drafters might well be between composing a statement of good intentions involving greater or lesser general commitments, or going, as is suggested in this paper, for mandatory obligations in some parts of the agreement and voluntary adherence to a code of good behavior in another. If the agreement were to have any meaning, it would be better to have relatively few but binding obligations and put contentious items into the code, than to emasculate the agreement as a whole.

International acceptance of even a few mandatory obligations would only be a beginning. In this field above all, where governments might be required to take unpopular action at home in response to unpopular pressure from abroad, there could be strong resistance to the decisions or recommendations of an international institution. What could be done in such cases short of sanctions or, in extreme circumstances, use of force? One ingenious idea, first put forward in 1974,[46] is for the establishment of a worldwide compensation scheme under which those ready to risk change, possibly against the advice of a majority of the scientific community, would agree beforehand to make reparation to others in certain defined circumstances if the worst occurred. This could be developed into a form of international insurance institution, funded by participating states, which would assess risks and fix premiums as in other forms of insurance. The prospect of a breath of cold actuarial air might itself give possible offenders pause.

But more powerful leverage might well be required, and it is hard to see how this could be exercised by an international institution except in special circumstances. Nor, to judge from recent history, could it be exercised by the great powers, who might well be at variance with each other or be among the offenders. However disagreeable it may sound, the countries or group of countries able to exercise leverage in this respect in the possible circumstances of the future are those who grow and export a surplus of foodstuffs, in particular grain. At present, this group includes Canada, the United States, Australia, and New Zealand, and could include the members of the European Community. It would be much easier and more generally acceptable if they were to exercise leverage to support the provisions of an international agreement than for motives which could be interpreted as selfish or designed to protect a position of advantage. This is an additional and powerful argument in favor of early negotiation of a wide-ranging agreement.

(4) International agreement to prevent the modification of the climate for purposes of war.

Twenty years ago the idea of an agreement to prevent

modification of the climate for military purposes would have been laughed out of court. Since then the war in Vietnam has greatly changed public attitudes, and an agreement to this effect is already the subject of international debate.

Beginning in 1963 and continuing until 1972, the United States experimented with various means of environmental warfare, ranging from defoliation of forests to modification of local weather. The results were generally below expectation. Such small-scale operations as seeding fog patches to clear runways or flight decks of aircraft carriers seem usually to have been successful; but attempts over five years to intensify normal monsoon rainfall so as to wash out North Vietnamese supply trails were of doubtful utility. It is also alleged that the Central Intelligence Agency tried to dry out the Cuban sugar crop by seeding clouds which would otherwise have brought rain to Cuba. Whether this was successful or not, the local weather is said to have been more erratic as a result.

Work on these techniques served to draw attention to other possibilities. An inventory of means of climatic among other sorts of environmental warfare makes frightening reading. It contains means of ruining crop and food supplies through creation of flood, drought, hail, or hurricane; swamping major cities and industries near sea level by stimulation of giant waves (tsunamis); striking at military targets with artificially induced lightning and at populations through interference with the electrical behavior of the ionosphere; and destructive irradiation of selected areas by blowing holes in the ozone layer. Some of these may be thought no worse than the use of nuclear weapons. That could be so. The effects of a major nuclear exchange might anyway be very similar. But climatic weapons would be much harder to control and the consequences could be forever irreversible.

News of the existence of this Pandora's box of horrors focused international attention on the need to keep the lid as tightly shut as possible. In December 1974 the United Nations General Assembly adopted Resolution No. 3264 (XXIX) entitled "Prohibition of action to influence the environment and climate for military and other purposes incompatible with the maintenance of international security, human well-being and health." In this Resolution it took note of a draft convention to this effect put forward by the Soviet Union, and requested the Conference of the Committee on Disarmament at Geneva to reach agreement on the text of a convention as soon as possible. The Soviet draft was wider in scope than was acceptable to the United States, and the two countries subsequently worked out a more limited text between them. Identical drafts were then submitted by these countries to the Committee on Disarmament in August 1975. In February 1976 both appealed for early international action on their draft.

The need for international agreement on this point speaks for itself. Even if the measure of agreement reached between the Soviet Union and the United States is relatively modest in scope, at least it represents a start. The conclusion of a treaty would greatly help negotiation of the wider international agreement suggested above.

The measures proposed may seem puny in relation to the problems we face. But even they present major difficulties, and agreement on them, or something like them, may not be feasible until the need becomes more manifest. By then it might be too late. Even if it were not too late, conditions might be worse than they are now, and the prospects for a rational world order more remote.

The most precious thing we have is the tiny, damp, curved space which is our living room. The pleasantly warm moment we now enjoy in it will not last forever. The room itself is changing, partly as a result of our actions, and we face intimidating responsibilities for it. We have no option but to meet them.

SUGGESTED READING
NOTES

SUGGESTED READING

Authorities have generally been quoted in numbered notes throughout this paper, and need not be repeated here. But the following were of particular value, and would serve as a general reading list.

H. H. Lamb: *Climate, Present, Past and Future:* Vol. 1. Methuen 1972.
US National Academy of Sciences: *Understanding Climatic Change.* 1975.
Report of the Study of Man's Impact on Climate: *Inadvertent Climate Modification.* M.I.T. 1971.
Nigel Calder: *The Weather Machine.* BBC 1974.
Proceedings of the SMC/IAMAP Symposium on *Long Term Climatic Fluctuations.* 1975.
Stephen H. Schneider: *The Genesis Strategy.* Plenum 1976.
Climatic Impact Assessment Program: Proceedings of successive Conferences. 1972 and 1974.
GARP Publications Series No. 16: *The Physical Basis of Climate and Climate Modelling.* 1975.
Report of Conference held at the Rockefeller Foundation: *Weather and Climate Change; Food Production and Interstate Conflict.* 1974.

NOTES

1. Reid A. Bryson, *A Perspective on Climatic Change* (Science, 1974), Vol. 184, p. 753.

2. R.W. Stewart, *The Atmosphere and the Ocean* (Scientific American, September 1969).

3. W.H. McCrae, Nature (1975), Vol. 255, p. 607.

4. G.E. Williams, Earth and Planetary Science Letters (1975), Vol. 26, p. 361.

5. Nigel Calder, *The Weather Machine* (1974), pp. 132-3.

6. H.H. Lamb, *Climate, Past, Present and Future* (1972), Vol. 1, pp. 14-67.

7. S.H. Schneider and C. Mass, *Volcanic Dust, Sunspots and Temperature Trends* (Science, 1975), Vol. 190, pp. 741-6.

8. John A. Eddy, *The Maunder Minimum* (February 1976), presented to the AAAS meeting, Boston.

9. Knud Frydendahl, *Variations in the Solar Intensity* (August 1975), paper presented to WMO/IAMAP Symposium, pp. 311-8.

10. A.B. Severny, V.A. Kotov and T.T. Tsap, *Observations of Solar Pulsations* (Nature, 15 January 1976), Vol. 259; J.R. Brookes, G.R. Isaak, and H.B. van der Raay, *Observation of Free Oscillations of the Sun* (Nature, 15 January 1976), Vol. 259; and John N. Bahcall and Raymond Davis Jr., *Solar Neutrinos: A Scientific Puzzle* (Science, 23 January 1976), Vol. 191.

11. H.H. Lamb, op. cit. (1972), pp. 212-53.

12. For full discussion of these themes see R.E. Newell, *Changes in the Poleward Energy Flux by the Atmosphere and Ocean as a Possible Cause for Ice Ages* (Quaternary Research, 1974), pp. 117-27; John Gribbin, *Antarctica Leads the Ice Ages* (New Scientist, 25 March 1976); and Nigel Calder, op. cit. (1974), pp. 102-5.

13. S.H. Schneider and Clifford Mass, op. cit. (1975).

14. Reid A. Bryson, op. cit. (1974).

15. H.H. Lamb, op. cit. (1972), pp. 410-35.

16. Nigel Calder, op. cit. (1974), pp. 24-8.

17. B.M. Gray, Weather (1975), Vol. 30.

18. U.S. National Academy of Sciences, *Understanding Climatic Change* (1975), pp. 24-8.

19. Report of the Study of Man's Impact on the Climate, *Inadvertent Climate Modification* (1971), M.I.T.

20. Stephen Schneider, *The Genesis Strategy* (1976), pp. 162-5.

21. Figure quoted by Erik Eckholm at meeting of the AAAS, Boston (February 1976).

22. Report of the Study of Man's Impact on Climate, op. cit. (1971), p. 13.

23. Howard A. Wilcox, *Hot House Earth* (1975), pp. 96-117.

24. For a full discussion of this subject, see Helmut Landsberg, *Inadvertent Atmospheric Modification through Urbanization* in *Weather and Climate Modification* (1974), ed. Wilmot N. Hess, pp. 726-63.

25. M.I. Budyko and I.L. Karol, *Man's Impact on the Global Climate* (August 1975), paper presented to WMO/IAMAP Symposium, pp. 465-71.

26. Ibid.

27. Ibid.

28. W.W. Kellogg, J.A. Coakley Jr. and G.W. Grams, *Effect of Anthropogenic Aerosols on the Global Climate* (August 1975), paper presented to WMO/IAMAP Symposium, pp. 323-7.

29. G.C. Reid, I.S.A. Isaksen, T.E. Holzer and P.J. Crutzen, *Influence of Ancient Solar-Proton Events on the Evolution of Life* (Nature, 1976), Vol. 259, pp. 177-9.

30. For a survey of the whole problem, see *Chlorofluorocarbons and their Effect on Stratospheric Ozone* (Department of the Environment: H.M. Stationery Office, 1976).

31. See the series of articles on *The Biological Effects of Climatic Change* in the Proceedings of the Third Conference of the Climatic Impact Assessment Program (U.S. Department of Transportation, March 1974, pp. 482-563).

32. Ronald Angione, Edward Medeiros and Robert Roosen, *Stratospheric Ozone as Viewed from the Chappuis Band* (Nature, 27 May 1976), Vols. 261 and 289.

33. A.V. Hill on The Ethical Dilemma of Science, quoted in Nature (1952), Vol. 170, pp. 388-93.

34. See for example the results of the meeting on Resource Development in Arid Lands organized by the Royal Society, London (March 1976).

35. U.S. National Academy of Sciences, op. cit. (1975), Appendix A, p. 143.

36. Nigel Calder, op. cit. (1974), pp. 130-8.

37. Howard A. Wilcox, op. cit. (1975), pp. 26-40.

38. See Derek Winstanley, *The Impact of Regional Climatic Fluctuations on Man: Some Global Implications* (August 1975), paper presented to WMO/IAMAP Symposium, pp. 479-90.

39. S. H. Schneider, op. cit. (1975), pp. 99-100, using statistics compiled by Lester Brown from data provided by the U.S. Department of Agriculture.

40. Mary McNeil, *Lateritic Soils* (November 1964), Scientific American.

41. For a particularly interesting discussion of some of these problems see Robert L. Heilbroner, *An Enquiry into the Human Prospect* (1974), Norton.

42. Report of the Study of Critical Environmental Problems, *Man's Impact on the Global Environment* (1970); and Report of the Study of Man's Impact on Climate (1971), op. cit.

43. Report of Conference on *Weather and Climate Change, Food Production and Interstate Conflict* (January 1974), Rockefeller Foundation, New York.

44. Report of the the Study of Man's Impact on Climate, op. cit. (1971), pp. 18-19 and 159-62.

45. M.I. Budyko and I.L. Karol, op. cit. (1975), pp. 465-70.

46. W.W. Kellogg and S.H. Schneider, *Climate Stabilization: For Better or Worse* (Science, 1974), Vol. 188, pp. 1163-73.

The Soviet Bloc, Zbigniew K. Brzezinski (sponsored jointly with the Russian Research Center), 1960. Harvard University Press. Revised edition, 1967.

The Necessity for Choice, by Henry A. Kissinger, 1961. Harper & Bros.

Rift and Revolt in Hungary, by Ferenc A. Váli, 1961. Harvard University Press.

Strategy and Arms Control, by Thomas C. Schelling and Morton H. Halperin, 1961. Twentieth Century Fund.

United States Manufacturing Investment in Brazil, by Lincoln Gordon and Engelbert L. Grommers, 1962. Harvard Business School.

The Economy of Cyprus, by A. J. Meyer, with Simos Vassiliou (sponsored jointly with the Center for Middle Eastern Studies), 1962. Harvard University Press.

Entrepreneurs of Lebanon, by Yusif A. Sayigh (sponsored jointly with the Center for Middle Eastern Studies), 1962. Harvard University Press.

Communist China 1955-1959: Policy Documents with Analysis, with a foreword by Robert R. Bowie and John K. Fairbank (sponsored jointly with the East Asian Research Center), 1962. Harvard University Press.

Somali Nationalism, by Saadia Touval, 1963. Harvard University Press.

The Dilemma of Mexico's Development, by Raymond Vernon, 1963. Harvard University Press.

Limited War in the Nuclear Age, by Morton H. Halperin, 1963. John Wiley & Sons.

In Search of France, by Stanley Hoffmann *et al.*, 1963. Harvard University Press.

The Arms Debate, by Robert A. Levine, 1963. Harvard University Press.

Africans on the Land, by Montague Yudelman, 1964. Harvard University Press.

Counterinsurgency Warfare, by David Galula, 1964. Frederick A. Praeger, Inc.

People and Policy in the Middle East, by Max Weston Thornburg, 1964. W. W. Norton & Co.

Shaping the Future, by Robert R. Bowie, 1964. Columbia University Press.

Foreign Aid and Foreign Policy, by Edward S. Mason (sponsored jointly with the Council on Foreign Relations), 1964. Harper & Row.

How Nations Negotiate, by Fred Charles Iklé, 1964. Harper & Row.

Public Policy and Private Enterprise in Mexico, edited by Raymond Vernon, 1964. Harvard University Press.

China and the Bomb, by Morton H. Halperin (sponsored jointly with the East Asian Research Center), 1965. Frederick A. Praeger, Inc.

Democracy in Germany, by Fritz Erler (Jodidi Lectures), 1965. Harvard University Press.

The Troubled Partnership, by Henry A. Kissinger (sponsored jointly with the Council on Foreign Relations), 1965. McGraw-Hill Book Co.

The Rise of Nationalism in Central Africa, by Robert I. Rotberg, 1965. Harvard University Press.

Pan-Africanism and East African Integration, by Joseph S. Nye, Jr., 1965.

Harvard University Press.

Communist China and Arms Control, by Morton H. Halperin and Dwight H. Perkins (sponsored jointly with the East Asian Research Center), 1965. Frederick A. Praeger, Inc.

Problems of National Strategy, ed. Henry Kissinger, 1965. Frederick A. Praeger, Inc.

Deterrence before Hiroshima: The Airpower Background of Modern Strategy, by George H. Quester, 1966. John Wiley & Sons.

Containing the Arms Race, by Jeremy J. Stone, 1966. M.I.T. Press.

Germany and the Atlantic Alliance: The Interaction of Strategy and Politics, by James L. Richardson, 1966. Harvard University Press.

Arms and Influence, by Thomas C. Schelling, 1966. Yale University Press.

Political Change in a West African State, by Martin Kilson, 1966. Harvard University Press.

Planning without Facts: Lessons in Resource Allocation from Nigeria's Development, by Wolfgang F. Stolper, 1966. Harvard University Press.

Export Instability and Economic Development, by Alasdair I. MacBean, 1966. Harvard University Press.

Foreign Policy and Democratic Politics, by Kenneth N. Waltz (sponsored jointly with the Institute of War and Peace Studies, Columbia University), 1967. Little, Brown & Co.

Contemporary Military Strategy, by Morton H. Halperin, 1967. Little, Brown & Co.

Sino-Soviet Relations and Arms Control, ed. Morton H. Halperin (sponsored jointly with the East Asian Research Center), 1967. M.I.T. Press.

Africa and United States Policy, by Rupert Emerson, 1967. Prentice-Hall.

Elites in Latin America, edited by Seymour M. Lipset and Aldo Solari, 1967. Oxford University Press.

Europe's Postwar Growth, by Charles P. Kindleberger, 1967. Harvard University Press.

The Rise and Decline of the Cold War, by Paul Seabury, 1967. Basic Books.

Student Politics, ed. S. M. Lipset, 1967. Basic Books.

Pakistan's Development: Social Goals and Private Incentives, by Gustav F. Papenek, 1967. Harvard University Press.

Strike a Blow and Die: A Narrative of Race Relations in Colonial Africa, by George Simeon Mwase, ed. Robert I. Rotberg, 1967. Harvard University Press.

Party Systems and Voter Alignments, edited by Seymour M. Lipset and Stein Rokkan, 1967. Free Press.

Agrarian Socialism, by Seymour M. Lipset, revised edition, 1968. Doubleday Anchor.

Aid, Influence, and Foreign Policy, by Joan M. Nelson, 1968. The Macmillan Company.

Development Policy: Theory and Practice, edited by Gustav F. Papanek, 1968. Harvard University Press.

International Regionalism, by Joseph S. Nye, 1968. Little, Brown & Co.

Revolution and Counterrevolution, by Seymour M. Lipset, 1968. Basic Books.

Political Order in Changing Societies, by Samuel P. Huntington, 1968.

Yale University Press.
The TFX Decision: McNamara and the Military, by Robert J. Art, 1968.
Little, Brown & Co.
Korea: The Politics of the Vortex, by Gregory Henderson, 1968. Harvard
University Press.
Political Development in Latin America, by Martin Needler, 1968. Random House.
The Precarious Republic, by Michael Hudson, 1968. Random House.
The Brazilian Capital Goods Industry, 1929-1964 (sponsored jointly with
the Center for Studies in Education and Development), by Nathaniel H.
Leff, 1968. Harvard University Press.
Economic Policy-Making and Development in Brazil, 1947-1964, by Nathaniel H. Leff, 1968. John Wiley & Sons.
Turmoil and Transition: Higher Education and Student Politics in India,
edited by Philip G. Altbach, 1968. Lalvani Publishing House (Bombay).
German Foreign Policy in Transition, by Karl Kaiser, 1968. Oxford University Press.
Protest and Power in Black Africa, edited by Robert I. Rotberg, 1969. Oxford University Press.
Peace in Europe, by Karl E. Birnbaum, 1969. Oxford University Press.
The Process of Modernization: An Annotated Bibliography on the Sociocultural Aspects of Development, by John Brode, 1969. Harvard University Press.
Students in Revolt, edited by Seymour M. Lipset and Philip G. Altbach,
1969. Houghton Mifflin.
*Agricultural Development in India's Districts: The Intensive Agricultural
Districts Programme*, by Dorris D. Brown, 1970. Harvard University
Press.
*Authoritarian Politics in Modern Society: The Dynamics of Established
One-Party Systems*, edited by Samuel P. Huntington and Clement H.
Moore, 1970. Basic Books.
Nuclear Diplomacy, by George H. Quester, 1970. Dunellen.
The Logic of Images in International Relations, by Robert Jervis, 1970.
Princeton University Press.
Europe's Would-Be Polity, by Leon Lindberg and Stuart A. Scheingold,
1970. Prentice-Hall.
Taxation and Development: Lessons from Colombian Experience, by Richard M. Bird, 1970. Harvard University Press.
Lord and Peasant in Peru: A Paradigm of Political and Social Change, by
F. LaMond Tullis, 1970. Harvard University Press.
The Kennedy Round in American Trade Policy: The Twilight of the GATT?
by John W. Evans, 1971. Harvard University Press.
Korean Development: The Interplay of Politics and Economics, by David
C. Cole and Princeton N. Lyman, 1971. Harvard University Press.
Development Policy II—The Pakistan Experience, edited by Walter P. Falcon and Gustav F. Papanek, 1971. Harvard University Press.
Higher Education in a Transitional Society, by Philip G. Altbach, 1971.
Sindhu Publications (Bombay).
Studies in Development Planning, edited by Hollis B. Chenery, 1971. Har-

vard University Press.

Passion and Politics, by Seymour M. Lipset with Gerald Schaflander, 1971. Little, Brown & Co.

Political Mobilization of the Venezuelan Peasant, by John D. Powell, 1971. Harvard University Press.

Higher Education in India, edited by Amrik Singh and Philip Altbach, 1971. Oxford University Press (Delhi).

The Myth of the Guerrilla, by J. Bowyer Bell, 1971. Blond (London) and Knopf (New York).

International Norms and War between States: Three Studies in International Politics, by Kjell Goldmann, 1971. Published jointly by Läromedelsförlagen (Sweden) and the Swedish Institute of International Affairs.

Peace in Parts: Integration and Conflict in Regional Organization, by Joseph S. Nye, Jr., 1971. Little, Brown & Co.

Sovereignty at Bay: The Multinational Spread of U.S. Enterprise, by Raymond Vernon, 1971. Basic Books.

Defense Strategy for the Seventies (revision of *Contemporary Military Strategy*), by Morton H. Halperin, 1971. Little, Brown & Co.

Peasants Against Politics: Rural Organization in Brittany, 1911-1967, by Suzanne Berger, 1972. Harvard University Press.

Transnational Relations and World Politics, edited by Robert O. Keohane and Joseph S. Nye, Jr., 1972. Harvard University Press.

Latin American University Students: A Six Nation Study, by Arthur Liebman, Kenneth N. Walker, and Myron Glazer, 1972. Harvard University Press.

The Politics of Land Reform in Chile, 1950-1970: Public Policy, Political Institutions and Social Change, by Robert R. Kaufman, 1972. Harvard University Press.

The Boundary Politics of Independent Africa, by Saadia Touval, 1972. Harvard University Press.

The Politics of Nonviolent Action, by Gene E. Sharp, 1973. Porter Sargent.

System 37 Viggen: Arms, Technology, and the Domestication of Glory, by Ingemar Dörfer, 1973. Universitetsforlaget (Oslo).

University Students and African Politics, by William John Hanna. 1974. Africana Publishing Company.

Organizing the Transnational: The Experience with Transnational Enterprise in Advanced Technology, by M. S. Hochmuth, 1974. Sijthoff (Leiden).

Becoming Modern, by Alex Inkeles and David H. Smith, 1974. Harvard University Press.

The United States and West Germany 1945-1973: A Study in Alliance Politics, by Roger Morgan (sponsored jointly with the Royal Institute of International Affairs), 1974. Oxford University Press.

Multinational Corporations and the Politics of Dependence: Copper in Chile, 1945-1973, by Theodore Moran, 1974. Princeton University Press.

The Andean Group: A Case Study in Economic Integration among Developing Countries, by David Morawetz, 1974. M.I.T. Press.

Kenya: The Politics of Participation and Control, by Henry Bienen, 1974. Princeton University Press.

Land Reform and Politics: A Comparative Analysis, by Hung-chao Tai, 1974. University of California Press.

Big Business and the State: Changing Relations in Western Europe, edited by Raymond Vernon, 1974. Harvard University Press.

Economic Policymaking in a Conflict Society: The Argentine Case, by Richard D. Mallon and Juan V. Sourrouille, 1975. Harvard University Press.

New States in the Modern World, edited by Martin Kilson, 1975. Harvard University Press.

Revolutionary Civil War: The Elements of Victory and Defeat, by David Wilkinson, 1975. Page-Ficklin Publications.

Politics and the Migrant Poor in Mexico City, by Wayne A. Cornelius, 1975. Stanford University Press.

East Africa and the Orient: Cultural Syntheses in Pre-Colonial Times, ed. H. Neville Chittick and Robert I. Rotberg, 1975. Africana Publishing Company.

No Easy Choice: Political Participation in Developing Countries, by Samuel P. Huntington and Joan M. Nelson, 1976. Harvard University Press.

The Politics of International Monetary Reform—The Exchange Crisis, by Michael J. Brenner, 1976. Ballinger Publishing Co.

The International Politics of Natural Resources, by Zuhayr Mikdashi, 1976. Cornell University Press.

The Oil Crisis, edited by Raymond Vernon, 1976. W. W. Norton & Co.

Social Change and Political Participation in Turkey, by Ergun Ozbudun, 1976. Princeton University Press.

The Arabs, Israelis, and Kissinger: A Secret History of American Diplomacy in the Middle East, by Edward R. F. Sheehan, 1976. Reader's Digest Press.

Perception and Misperception in International Politics, by Robert Jervis, 1976. Princeton University Press.

Power and Interdependence, by Robert O. Keohane and Joseph S. Nye, Jr., 1977. Little, Brown.

Soldiers in Politics: Military Coups and Governments, by Eric Nordlinger, 1977. Prentice-Hall.

The Military and Politics in Modern Times: On Professionals, Praetorians, and Revolutionary Soldiers, by Amos Perlmutter, 1977. Yale University Press.

Raw Materials Investments and American Foreign Policy, by Stephen D. Krasner, 1977. Princeton University Press.

Bankers and Borders: The Case of the American Banks in Britain, by Janet Kelly, 1977. Ballinger Publishing Co.

Shattered Peace: The Origins of the Cold War and the National Security State, by Daniel Yergin, 1977. Houghton Mifflin.

Storm Over the Multinationals: The Real Issues, by Raymond Vernon, 1977. Harvard University Press.

HARVARD STUDIES IN INTERNATIONAL AFFAIRS*

[formerly Occasional Papers in International Affairs]

*Available from Harvard University Center for International Affairs, 6 Divinity Avenue, Cambridge, Massachusetts 02138
†Out of print. Reprints may be ordered from AMS Press, Inc., 56 East 13th Street, New York, N.Y. 10003

†21. *Internal War and International Systems: Perspectives on Method*, by George A. Kelley and Linda B. Miller, 1969.

†22. *Migrants, Urban Poverty, and Instability in Developing Nations*, by Joan M. Nelson, 1969. 81 pp.

23. *Growth and Development in Pakistan, 1955-1969*, by Joseph J. Stern and Walter P. Falcon, 1970. 94 pp. $3.50.

24. *Higher Education in Developing Countries: A Select Bibliography*, by Philip G. Altbach, 1970. 118 pp. $4.50.

25. *Anatomy of Political Institutionalization: The Case of Israel and Some Comparative Analyses*, by Amos Perlmutter, 1970. 60 pp. $2.95.

†26. *The German Democratic Republic from the Sixties to the Seventies*, by Peter Christian Ludz, 1970. 100 pp.

27. *The Law in Political Integration: The Evolution and Integrative Implications of Regional Legal Processes in the European Community*, by Stuart A. Scheingold, 1971. 63 pp. $2.95.

28. *Psychological Dimensions of U.S.-Japanese Relations*, by Hiroshi Kitamura, 1971. 46 pp. $2.50.

29. *Conflict Regulation in Divided Societies*, by Eric A. Nordlinger, 1972. 142 pp. $4.95.

30. *Israel's Political-Military Doctrine*, by Michael I. Handel, 1973. 101 pp. $3.75.

31. *Italy, NATO, and the European Community: The Interplay of Foreign Policy and Domestic Politics*, by Primo Vannicelli, 1974. 67 + x pp. $3.75.

32. *The Choice of Technology in Developing Countries: Some Cautionary Tales*, by C. Peter Timmer, John W. Thomas, Louis T. Wells, Jr., and David Morawetz, 1975. 114 pp. $3.95.

33. *The International Role of the Communist Parties of Italy and France*, by Donald L. M. Blackmer and Annie Kriegel, 1975. 67 + x pp. $3.50.

34. *The Hazards of Peace: A European View of Detente*, by Juan Cassiers, 1976. 94 pp. $6.95, cloth; $3.50, paper.

35. *Oil and the Middle East War: Europe in the Energy Crisis*, by Robert J. Lieber, 1976. 75 + x pp. $7.45, cloth; $3.45, paper.

36. *Foreign Policy and the American Voter*, by William Schneider, 1977.

37. *Climatic Change and World Affairs*, by Crispin Tickell, 1977. 78 pp. $8.95, cloth; $3.95, paper.